Sometimes
in Life,
It Happens..!!

Sometimes in Life, It Happens..!!

A Fight for His Future ..
A Fight for His True Love ..

Nikunj Khatri

PARTRIDGE
A Penguin Random House Company

To order additional copies of this book, contact
Partridge India
000 800 10062 62
orders.india@partridgepublishing.com

www.partridgepublishing.com/india

Contents

To my beloved sister Gayatri Khatri, who was always there with me in my every big decision. Thank you Didi for your support. You are more than my mom to me.

These two thoughts I always kept in my mind while writing this novel.

"The most interesting thing about writing a novel is that you don't have to be true to the real world but only to the story."

"Sometimes the best way to express how you feel is to find the song with the perfect lyrics."

Acknowledgement

First of all I would like to thank my publisher, **Partridge Publishers**, who trusted me and gave me an opportunity to prove myself. Thank you so much, Samuel Sagario, without your help & trust on me, this work had remained just in paper, it won't become a book.

A great thank you to my brother in law **Mahendra Khatri** & Brother **Suresh Dholwani** for supporting financially in every manner they could.

I would like to thank my cousins **Tarun Khatri** and **Namrata Khatri** for guiding me through the ways of Ahmedabad and **Garima Bakshi** for guiding through the ways of Pune and Bangalore.

A special thanks to my friend **Ankita Mathur** who helped me in editing this book. Thank you for the same to **Rudra Traders.**

I would like to thank my cousin **Meghna Khatri** for sharing her beautiful poems with me. Then I would like to thank my friends Priyanka Panwar, Nancy Verma, Kaynat Quadri, Aabshar Quadri, Rashmi Aswani, Mohini Singh, Jyoti Shekhawat, Anjali Choudhary, Anu Choudhary, Lubna Khan,

Neha Bhutra, Parneet Kaur, Nitu Ramani, and all my colleagues and batch mates for their guidance, help and moral support to complete this work.

I thank all my maternal and paternal cousins for encouraging me a lot.

Last but not the least I would like to thank all those lyricists whose songs I have used in this book.

Author's Note

Have you ever fallen in Love? Nothing feels better than finding someone you always dream of and falling in love with the same. Finding a perfect partner who is always there for you whatever may be the circumstances, is the lucky part of yours. Love makes one stable, the life gets its meaning, destiny gets it definition, the air around gets fragranced, the sun is no warmer, and the moon & stars are the most beautiful things of the world. Many of us may or may not believe in Love. But if you ask me, I believe in Love. There is something called Love, but there is nothing to explain in it. No definition exists for love. It's just the purest feeling between the two hearts. And those people are very lucky who experience this purest feeling in their hearts. Love is when you look into someone's eyes and see everything you need. Love doesn't happen with planning. It just happens and brings out a tremendous change in one's life. To get a life partner who understands you so well, can listen to your unsaid words, can see your love in your eyes, always hold your hand and wish to be with you forever, this phase of life is that where you have achieved everything. If you look close enough to the world around you, you might find someone like you, someone trying to find their way, someone trying to find their self. Sometimes, it seems like you are the only one in the world who's struggling, who's frustrated, unsatisfied, barely getting by. But that feeling's a lie. And if you just hold on, just find the courage to face it all for another day, someone or something will find you and make it all okay, because we all need a little help sometimes. We need someone to remind us that it won't always be this way. That someone is out there. And that someone will find you.

"Sometimes in Life, it Happens!" is a story of Arhaan Kashyap, a middle class boy, who suffered from an Indian castism i.e. Reservation.

After 65 years of Independence, some of us don't have freedom to choose our career. May be Dr. Ambedkar knew what was good for the developing India then, maybe he succeeded in bringing the country to where it is now, but not at the cost of abolishing deserving (general) candidates. It's not only Arhaan, but thousands of deserving candidates every year have to bestow their seats to some students out of which some don't even meet the criteria or condition that are needed to secure those reserved seats. Many aspirants who live in suitable (favourable) conditions & have all amenities & environment required studying peacefully, misusing this quota even then they obtain less marks. This is clear abuse to our fundamental right i.e., Right to Equality.

1

It was morning 07:30. The alarm was ringing on the table beside my bed. I removed the blanket from my face and turned it off and got up with a yawn while wearing my slippers. I went to the washroom to get ready for my monotonous office life.

I locked my flat and moved down towards my car. On the way of my office I tuned the FM radio, which was playing "bin tere, bin tere, bin tere koi khalish hai hawayo mein bin tere..."

Each and every gloomy song reminds me of Aaliya. Somebody has said very true "After breakup it seems every sad song is made for you. In love you enjoy the love songs and after breakup you actually understand the lyrics."

I entered the gate of my office. My workplace is 'Accentia Marketing Media'. I live in Pune and working as the legal adviser here since last 10 months. I took the keys of my cabin from the reception and proceeded towards the lift. On reaching my cabin I relaxed myself on the chair and turned on my laptop. I was going through all the notifications and messages on Facebook, Gmail and twitter. After that I checked my meeting schedule for the present date. No work at all for today, I was free for the whole day. It was useless to spend the whole day in office so I took permission from my boss to leave. He agreed and I left the office and called Samarth and Faizan at conference and asked their schedule. Awesome they are free too. We planned to meet at bar. We usually meet in a bar where we share our funny stories, drink and smoke for hours.

While I was on my way, I saw a flower shop. There was a large bouquet of red roses kept there. In morning the song reminded me of Aaliya and now these red roses.

She loved the fragrance of red roses and I loved her's. I thought to buy that so I stopped my car and went to that flower shop. I asked the lady standing there for its cost. It cost Rs 450. I paid for it and kept it at the back seat of my car. I thought for whom did I buy this? The person who loved the red roses so much is not even the part of my life now. So many past memories were attached with red roses. The day when I proposed Aaliya, I have bought red roses for her. That thought made me smile, but it was useless to remember past. Past is a very good place to visit but not at all good to stay.

But still, my mind has already entered in flashback. All those questions were again hitting my soul. Why did she leave me without giving a genuine reason for breakup? She even broke our engagement. In my thoughts don't know when but I reached the bar. They both were waiting for me in the parking area. I locked my car and went towards them. We had a high five and entered the bar. We ordered a full mug of beer. Whenever Aaliya hits my mind I drink a lot. They both were enjoying but I was lost in my past.

None other than Aaliya was hitting my mind all the time while I was in bar. Very soon their girlfriends Naina and Sara too reached there. All four were enjoying but I left the place without saying anything to anyone.

Those roses disturbed my mind. I sat in my car drove somewhere to infinity, don't know where to go. I was just driving to somewhere. My phone was ringing it was bhaiya. I picked up, he said, "hello Arhaan where are you?" I said bhaiya I am going to office. I am on the way". Yeah I lied. He said "okay reach your office and then talk to me. There's something important for you to know." I said, "Ok bhaiya". He then disconnected the call.

As soon as I kept the phone, it again rang and it was Samarth this time. He said betraying, "Where are you? Why you left so early, without saying anything to anyone? Are you alright?" I said, "Yes I am. Actually a call came from office so I had to leave urgently." Yeah I again lied. To two people I have said that I am going to office but I was going nowhere. My friends are too caring when it comes to me. They can understand the awkward feeling in me when they enjoy all the get-togethers and parties with their girlfriends and I stand all alone there watching all couples enjoying.

Samarth scoffed, "You bloody liar; I know whenever you drink too much, Aaliya hits your mind and heart. I know you will be going central park to take yourself towards your so called past." and he disconnected the call.

Samarth was my closest friend. He knows my each and every secret, my top secrets my deep dug secrets. We met in 11th standard. We completed our schooling together. I turned my car and now finally decided to go central park. When I was on my way, I saw a huge crowd, I saw boards in their hands shouting "reservation must be banned", "all must get equal rights for their education", "remove this law", "government is doing cheating with general students".

Seeing this I remembered those days of my post school vacation. When I was preparing for my admission in NLU, I dropped one year to prepare for CLAT. I prepared hard. We four, Samarth, Faizan, Shaurya and I, had prepared very much. We studied together waking up for so many nights. But when exam result was declared only Faizan and Shaurya cleared it. Samarth and I could not clear it just because we scored 4 marks less than the cut-off score. We inquired a lot and found that there are still few seats left vacant. We applied through management but our forms were rejected because those seats are only reserved for SC/ST.

They say our friends from backward classes are facing hardships and find it difficult to educate themselves. Well, then why make it difficult to educate them? Why make it difficult for us? Don't we have to give the same challenging exam? Don't we study for twelve hours straight starting at 4 in the morning? Don't we deserve seat that we worked equally or even harder for?

Well, it's now useless to think over this. I suffered a lot and finally won the war. These people also have to fight to get what they wish.

I moved my car out of that crowd and reached the central park. I parked my car and moved inside. The frustration of those hard days was making my blood pressure high. I took 2 cans of beer out from my car and went inside to sit peacefully somewhere.

I haven't got admission in NLU and neither Samarth so we decided to do BBA from some other college. We took admission in BBA college of Ahmedabad in July. The place where I was forced to go but that place only gave me Aaliya. 1 can of beer fully inside me took me to the past. The day when I saw her for the first time, the day *Jab we met* for the first time.

2

It was 15 July- my birthday. Those days I used to live in Ahmedabad. I was there for my BBA graduation course. I used to live in boys hostel along with Samarth. That morning I woke up early. I was standing in balcony and was planning my day. Suddenly I saw a girl who was standing in the balcony of the opposite hostel (girls' hostel).

She was standing all alone. I infer she was also planning her day like me. I didn't know her but she was attractive. Her face was calm and her sweet smile made me unable to put my eyes off her. I never felt like this before what I felt seeing her.

It was like some magnetic force that was attracting me towards her. I wish I could make a bridge between the two balconies and go to see her very closely. I was observing her but after sometime she went inside. I really got upset then I too went inside and got to attend the very 1st lecture of the day. The day was very special day for me. I dint want to ruin this day by attending accounts lecture but I had to.

I rushed towards lecture hall as I was already late. I was searching a vacant seat but I couldn't find any. Suddenly I saw the same girl, sitting alone on a seat of two, and my heart started beating vigorously, I went to sit beside her. I thought to talk to her but at first I hesitated a little. After sometime said a "hi" formally, she replied same with a beautiful smile. Wow! What a smile she passed. I almost got bowled over it. LOL, really very pretty smile. I then asked her, "Is it your first class here?"

She said, "Yes"

I said, "Then you must be lagging behind too much, the session started 2 weeks earlier on 1st July. She said, "Ya I know. I need to complete my left units as early as possible" I said, "Yes you must! The exams have been organized so early in this session. Probably they are 50 days later."

She said, "Oh my god, really!" I just have 50 days!" She got tensed but 50 days are more than enough.

I said, "You don't worry. I will help you out. You take my notes and return them when you cover up all." The tension decreased a little bit and she said, "So nice of you. Thank you so much."

I thought that it was a great chance to stand up for friendship. Damn! She was pretty, her pretty face and sweet smile. *It was a perfect combination of qualities for a perfect girl.* I was clean bowled. That day I was completely exited. In the morning I wasn't willing to attend the lectures but now I think that if I hadn't come here to attend the lecture then I would have missed the chance to meet her. Now I could spend the whole day here if she sits beside me.

She asked, "By the way, what's your name?" I looked at her, gave a smile, "Arhaan. **Arhaan Kashyap.**" After a pause, I asked her name. She smiled and replied, "**Aaliya Juneja**".

I thought Aaliya was really a lovely name. But what's the meaning of Aaliya? Then I thought what I have to do with the meaning of her name. I even don't know the meaning of Arhaan itself. We spent six hours together that day. I explained her everything related to college and all related to classes and lectures. Those six hours were like a birthday gift from God. In morning when I saw her first time I wished I could meet her just once and God did that for me. Wow, what a lovely time it was. Her smile has overridden my senses. For the next ten days I helped her a lot in completing her left portion and within ten days we became very good friends. I used to sing a song in bathroom daily."Pehli nazar mein kaisa jaadu kar diya, Tera bann baitha hai mera jiya"

One day Samarth caught me when I was sitting alone and smiling. He slapped my forehead and asked, "Have you gone mad?" I forgot to tell him about Aaliya. I said very excitedly, "Hey man, I met one girl." He laughed and asked, "Where, in your class?" I said, "Yes. Her name is Aaliya. What a beautiful girl she is. And what a pretty smile she owns." He asked, "So, you are in love with her?"

I gave a weird look to him and said, "Nah. I don't believe in love at first sight. But she is attractive. Love takes a lot of time to happen. Love is not a matter of what happens in life. It's matter of what's happening in your heart. The moment you have in your heart this extraordinary thing called love and feel the depth, the delight, the ecstasy of it you will discover that for you the world is transformed." Samarth was staring at me with his eyes opened wide. He then said, "Bas, finish this love pravachann for today and let's go for dinner otherwise the mess will be closed, Come on, let's move." We both went for dinner.

We both went for dinner. After returning, had some chitchat of the whole day, the mimicry of the teachers, made fun of everybody whom we met that day and slept around 12:30 am.

3

As we were good friends now, we exchanged our phone numbers too. We used to share our thoughts. One day, during our free time, we were sitting in the garden beside mess. She was telling about herself and her family. She was saying, "I always wished to live a life full of freedom and parents never determent me in any decision. But I never misused the freedom they gave me. I always remained in my limits. I know my limits but I seriously don't know how to cross them." I laughed and said, "Same here. I too wished to live a life but my parents never supported me in anything. They made me a puppet of their dreams." I was getting aggressive so I stopped myself and asked, "Your family includes how many members?" She said, "There is my mom, my dad and an elder sister who is about to get married." I said, "Oh that's cool." She asked, "You tell me about your family?" I got little upset but I didn't want to tell her about my family. She said, "Come on, say." I finally said, "In my family, there is my elder brother, my bhabhi and one small nephew Rohan. That's it." She said, "Oh good and what about your parents?" Some tears rolled down from my eyes and then I said, "They passed away last year in an accident." I then wiped my tears. Then she said, "Oh I'm sorry." Then she held my hand to console me. For the first time I felt her touch, her soft fingers. She tried to change the atmosphere, "You know I belong to Nasik. My parents live there only. Where your brother lives?" I said, "He lives in Bangalore. He's a software engineer. Earlier we used to live in Ahmedabad with mom and dad in our own house." 2 years back, my brother left the house and settled in Bangalore after he had a huge fight with dad. She said, "Fight with your dad, but why? What happened?"

I explained her, "Actually dad never gave any kind of freedom to my brother. He made my brother his puppet. Whatever dad said, that has to be done by him. Otherwise dad used to condemn him. He suffered a lot during his student life. Really, dad used to do a lot of "Emotional Attyachar" on him and the same way he behaved with me. My brother tolerated all this quietly and I always used to protest this. Even my brother hasn't chosen the career of his choice. He wanted to be in the field of law but dad forced him to be an engineer. I must appreciate my brother, whatever maybe the circumstances, whether he wished to do or not, whatever dad asked him to do, he always fulfilled his wishes. And I was always unable to do that. Dad used to scold both of us a lot. His nature was annoying, he always remained frustrated. Dad had not changed even after my brother's marriage. My brother's tolerance power now crossed the limit and he decided to live separately so he settled his own turf in Bangalore and if you ask about me I have never decided that what I have to do in my life. But when my brother left our home, that day

I sensed a kind of responsibility in me, for his sake I decided to go in the field of law. Last year mom and dad have decided to apologize in front of my brother and bring him back. So they left for Bangalore to visit him. I was so happy to know that bhaiya will come back home with bhabhi. But unfortunately mom and dad met with an accident while they were on their way to Bangalore." I paused and tears were rolling down from eyes. This time she wiped my tears and embraced me. I held her tight and her warm hug made me calm down. I then handled myself. It was evening and time for our dinner so we went to mess. Outside mess Samarth met me and asked, "Where were you for the whole day? I called so many times, but you did not pick" I said nothing; he read my face and said "you seem to be upset. What happened?" I said lets have dinner and then I'll tell you." We went inside for dinner. I hate this mess food. The vegetables were boiled and there was just a pinch of spices in it as if this is not a college mess, it is a hospital mess. Not even onion and garlic in any vegetable. I love to eat onion. At home, I don't go near the food till the smell of onion attracts me. I can eat onion dishes everyday whether it is pyaaz parathans or pyaaz pakodas, pyaaz ki sabji or a simple onion salted with lemon and a chapatti. But I was helpless to eat that food for my survival. Every Sunday we three friends went out for our lunch and dinner. This time Aaliya was also with me and Samarth on outing. If you visit Ahmedabad and never ate "Wada Paav" that means you wasted your time in Ahmedabad. Aaliya has never tasted that, we made her to eat that, it was little spicy but she liked it very much. ☺

4

I suddenly realized that it was evening now and I am sitting here since afternoon. There were so many missed calls and messages from different people. I checked the messages one was of Naina. Naina is Samarth's girlfriend, who met him through a wrong number. Coincidently they met during our graduation in Ahmadabad. She was my friend too. We used to share our feelings with each other. I read her message, "Where are you? You left from bar also so early? Are you alright?"

I replied here, "Yes I am fine. Not to worry. I was busy in office with a client."

She replied, "Oh Arhaan, I messaged you at 4pm and now it's 8."

I replied, "Yes, I told you I was busy, now leaving for home."

She replied, "Okay go home. Have your dinner properly and take rest. You do lots of work."

I replied, "Okay. Surely I will ☺"

She replied, "Mom calling for dinner. Bye."

I went to parking picked up my car and moved out of the car lot. On my way to home I bought few packets of cigarette. I reached home. I was not hungry at all. I straight went into my bedroom changed my clothes and rested myself on bed. I took one cigarette and lighted it. In the smoke of cigarette I could see image of Aaliya. First she went deep inside me and then moved out and disappeared like this smoke. After smoking few cigarettes and seeing her all the pictures that I have I slept. Don't know when I fell asleep but when I woke up it was morning 7am. I brushed my teeth and then prepared tea for myself. The morning was bit cold due to rainy season. Monsoon has reached Pune. I checked my newspaper while having tea. My newspaper was not that ordinary one. My newspaper was Facebook. I was addicted to Facebook too much. I use to update lots of status everyday & my friends always ruin my feelings by their stupid comments. I ignored those. I was finished with my tea so went for shower. I came out of shower and opened my wardrobe. Aaliya always used to say black suits me. So, I wore black shirt along with blue jeans and white blazer. I moved out of my house & headed towards the office. I had my breakfast in office canteen. After that I checked my schedule, no appointments, no meetings, and no clients. Another free day, I stared at Aaliya's pic which was on my table. I then took my notepad & wished to write something for her. Thoughts were coming in my mind & then those thoughts turned into words:

"*Sometimes I feel like my need to see you, is consuming me inside & sometimes when I think about you, I tremble my love for you is never easy to hide. I called my best friend to explain how much I love you, but the words stalled on my tongue & again I pretend because I can't tell a picture I love you. I don't know what I want in my life. I don't know what I want right now. All I know is that I'm hurting so much inside, that it's eating me & one day there won't be any more of me left. Everything that ever causes a tear to tickles down my cheeks. I run away & hide from it. But now everything is unwinding & finding its way back towards me. And I don't know what to do. I just know the pain I felt so long ago; it's hurting ten times more."*

My eyes were wet; I got up from my seat & in hurry went outside the office. My heart was saying, go, go & search her everywhere. Search in the whole world, where ever she is. Just go & find her. I was approaching my car, and then I sat inside. Then I realised from where I would start searching, where is she? I don't know anything about her. I was feeling like to die. But no, I want her back & I will. I started my car & drove it towards the central park again, the only place where I share my loneliness. I reached the park & sat on the same place as I was on yesterday. I sat to relaxed myself & smoked 2 cigarettes. Aaliya was ruling my mind, my heart, my soul. I was getting mad, crazy!! I wanted to see her like one needs air to breathe. I was now again recalling my past. The moment when I realised that we stepped on the next level of friendship.

#5

That day she came to class, but was looking upset. I said "Hi". She replied with same but in a very low voice. Her usual sweet smile was missing somewhere.

I asked," What happened? You looking tensed."

She said. "I have lost my assignment two days back. I searched it everywhere but haven't found yet. It was a bit incomplete too. Now I don't know what to do? I worked hard on that but look at my misfortune. I lost it two days ago and haven't got the time to do it again that was of 36 pages. She threw her bag on the seat & sat there. She was very much upset. Sir entered the class & was asking everyone individually about their assignment. Her facial expressions were getting more & more stressed. I took out my assignment from my bag& said to her, "Here's your assignment." She was shocked to see that. She opened it & said, "It's not my assignment. It's not my handwriting even. It's yours. I know your handwriting. Take it back. I won't let you in trouble for me.

I said. "Take this, I will show you a magic. Give it to sir." She asked, "Then what will you submit?" Till then sir has reached us & asked Aaliya to submit her assignment. She looked at me & I told her to submit. She gave; sir saw and appreciated the work. Now it was my turn. I took out one more file and gave it to sir. Sir checked it and moved further. Aaliya was staring at me with a shock. "You did assignment twice? Did you see a dream that I am going to lose my assignment or what?" I laughed loud & said, "No I found your assignment on a bench in garden day before yesterday. Probably you have forgotten it there. I took it & kept it with me. I saw it & found bit incomplete so I completed it too. Yesterday I was about to return it to you, but then I thought to have some fun with you so I kept it with me only. See I saved you today."

She was getting a mixed feeling of relief and anger. She said," I don't know whether to thank you for completing it or to beat you hard for hiding this from me from last two days." I laughed and said, "Thanking me is much better option." She laughed too. I love it when she laughs & her hair fall on her face. So softly, so calmly she used her finger to keep them at the back of her ear. The college got over. We came out of the class together & went to the campus garden. We sat there on the bench. I took a deep breathe of the fresh air from the surroundings. We looked at each other and smiled. I said, "Sorry." She asked, "Why sorry? Please don't be. The most important thing was to submit the assignment, nothing else. And you did that."

I said, "Then also, I am just a friend of yours. May be you have felt bad that how could I do such a prank regarding the assignment." She said holding my hand, "It's alright. You are a good friend of mine. You can prank with me anytime."

I took a breath of relief. She said GOOD FRIENDS!! Wow ....

I then asked her, "So what's your plan after completing BBA?" She said, "Umm I am thinking to pursue MBA from Mumbai and after that definitely a good job." I said, "Wow, that's great. And what about marriage, Love or arrange?" Oops..!! Why I am asking this to her. It's too personal. She gave me a weird look & said, "Love marriage, but only if my parents approve that man." I hope she hasn't mind asking such questions. Then she asked, "So, what's your future plans?" I said, "Actually I wanted to get admission in NLU. I dropped my one year to prepare for CLAT. But unfortunately, all seats were full at the time of my admission. So now I am thinking to do LLB from Pune in future and same, after that a good job. I want to earn lots of money & return it to my brother. He did a lot for me and he has lots of expectation from me as well. And I have to fulfil each one of them anyhow." She said, "Good and what about your marriage?" Her clear emphasis was on YOUR. And that made me smile. I said, "Marriage, after getting a job & earning lots of money, and yes of course Love marriage.

Suddenly a grasshopper came and sat on her shoulder. She saw it & started jumping & screaming. I removed that from her shoulder & she suddenly hugged me as she was so much scared. I was laughing seeing her coward face. But when she hugged me an immense feeling I felt in my heart. I tried to calm down her, "Don't scream, the grasshopper is getting scared. She moved back & said, "You can see the grasshopper scaring, can't you see my condition." I laughed and said, "Calm down, it's not going to bite you or kill you. It's just a small grasshopper not a dinosaur. The time when she was in my arms holding my shirt very tightly I really skipped my heart beat. Her coward facing was looking so cute, her eyes, her nose, truly amazing. I wish I could capture her each & every expression. She was looking like a small 5 year old girl, who has seen an insect & was hiding herself from it so that it could not harm her.

She said, "Ok now, I have to go to my room. Mummy's call is about to come." I said, "Ok Bye." That grasshopper was still there in the grass. I went a bit closer to it and said, "Thank you my friend." and gave a flying kiss to it. "I wish I could keep you as my pet so that every day I can keep you on her shoulder and she gets scared every day. And every day, I will get a hug from her." I tried to touch it and hold in my hand, but it shook itself in such a way that this time I fell on ground because I got scared. I didn't know Aaliya was standing at a distance and was still seeing me. She saw me falling on ground. She burst out in laugh and said, "Stupid." I laughed at myself. I came to my room. That evening I was thinking about her only. Her innocent face, her eyes, these all were roaming around my eyes. My ears were able to hear only her sweet voice, nothing else. I was again smiling like an idiot & this time too Samarth caught me.

He said, "Now what?? You proposed her?"

I said, "No you dumb.

He asked, "Then why smiling like an idiot lover?"

I took a deep breath and can smell an immense fragrance everywhere around me. I said, "Dude, you know how beautiful she is. Her smile is the most beautiful smile & I skip my heart beat when she smiles. She is just like an angel. Her smile always tries to override my senses. I love her to see in long untied hair, that fall on her eyes with a gust of wind. Her body appears so perfect, so young, so poised. She is charismatic. I am always unable to flake my eyes off from her. I can stare her for my whole life. I feel an immense fragrance all around when I take a deep breathe."

Samarth was looking at me. He said, "OMG!! Dude you are gone. Congrats man, you are in Love with her." I gave a weird look, "No, that's not possible. Love doesn't happen so easy and so early. It takes lot of time to happen. We are just good friends." He said, "I bet, that you are in love with her & soon you will realise this, come to me that day."

I laughed and we both slept then. Samarth was snoring whole night, and I, I could not sleep the whole night. I thought about Aaliya. Why this all was happening with me. Am I really in love with her?" Then my mind said, "How this is possible. No you are not in love with her." But my heart denied it and said, "Why no, yes, you are in love with her. Anybody can fall in love. Anywhere you can fall in love. The whole night my mind & my heart had a great debate. Finally I decided to observe the symptoms of falling in love within myself.

#6

I have smoked almost 16 cigarettes & then got my senses. It was evening I was still laying restless in the park on the bench. A hit from a football from a small kid came to me and took me out of my past. The small kid came to me and took the ball saying sorry. I stood up from there & moved out. I checked my phone, 3 missed calls from Faizan. 1 missed call from Samarth, 2 missed calls from Shaurya. I called Samarth. He picked up the call & shouted, "Where the hell are you since afternoon. We all called you so many times. I said, "Ya I just saw my phone. Say what happened?" He said, "Naina invited all of us on dinner tonight, so come at 9pm at her house." I checked my watch, it was already 7pm, "Ok, I will be there, by the way who all are invited?" He said, "You, me, Shaurya, Sarah, Faizan, Rumana." I said, "Ok, after a long time we all will be together, great. I will be there on time."

I went home and then I saw myself in mirror. What has happened to me? Few years back there was a time when I can't stop smiling & now I am dying to smile. Nothing makes me happy. I was starving as if Aaliya is my only food. My head was bursting in her thoughts. Where the hell she is? Why she left me? I still don't know. All these questions echo in my mind every day. I wish to hit the mirror hard, but useless. I then went to take bath. I got ready for the dinner and went to Naina's house. As per before mentioned Naina is Samarth's girlfriend and my close friend too. Though I came to know her through Samarth only but few months ago when they broke up for some time, in those days I consoled her lot. I solved their matter too. Actually I do solve everybody's matter. All these six people call me their love Guru. Strange, their Love Guru's love life is almost screwed. Well, I reached Naina's home. She lives in her house with her parents. I wished them & then joined my gang in her room upstairs. They all were already there & even started enjoying. All those committed people were discussing their weddings. When to get marry? How to get marry? Where to get marry? As they saw me, they all shouted, "OMG, Arhaan!!"

I said, "What??"

Samarth said in my ear, "Dude, you wore track pant instead of jeans under the shirt and blazer." They all burst out in laugh & I saw downwards. "Oh Fish..!! I was really wearing track pant which I usually wear after my evening bath. Such a fool I am! I removed my blazer, and then I was looking bit normal. They all were still laughing at me & I was feeling so embarrassed. Faizan said, "It's alright dude, chill. Sometimes in life it happens...!"

Naina's maid has brought dinner for us. We all had dinner, gossiped a lot, and enjoyed a lot. After so many days I laughed that much. But sometimes I just wanna stay alone, all alone. Like an isolated creature. The girls decided to have a night stay at Naina's place. We all four boys decided to go for drinks. We all went in Samarth's car, bought lots of cans of beer, and few bottles of rum. The time was around 1 am, all around complete silence. Faizan, Shaurya & Samarth came to me & asked, "For how much time, you wanna wait for her, now at least find another girl and get settled." I said, "I am not waiting for her. Actually I cannot handle any other girl in my life. She is the only girl who can live in my heart. I can't even imagine any other girl in place of her. Love happen only once, and if happens twice, then your first love was never true. My love for Aaliya is still true and will remain such always. I don't know whether she will be back or not, but nobody can ever replace her in my heart, my mind, in my soul. Samarth said, "You are seriously mad."

After having lots of drinks, Samarth dropped each one of us to our respective places. The time was 3.30 am. The next day was Sunday. I was so tired so I fell on my bed restlessly and slept soon. The next morning I got up with a phone call from bhabhi. I saw the time, it was 10.15 am. I picked up the call. Talked to bhabhi for a while & then I got fresh. After making tea for myself, I turned on my laptop. There were so many pictures of Aaliya in my laptop. Aaliya.. Aaliya.. From past 3 days why she is hitting my mind again & again. What kind of intuitions are these. I never thought this much about here in past one & half year. Our one pic reminded me that incident which made me realise that I seriously feel something for her. She really made a special place in my heart.

7

One day when I went into the lecture hall. I saw Aaliya talking to one guy. I silently went upwards to capture my seat. She finished her talking. I turned around. She saw me & came upwards to sit beside me. She smiled & said, "Hi" I replied in a very low pitch. "Hi". I haven't looked into her eyes. Her smile also was not so killing like every day or may be due to jealousy. I haven't found it killing. She noticed that something is wrong with me. She asked me. "What happened? Are you upset? I said, again rudely. Nothing Leave."

She said, "No something is wrong. Tell me. What's the problem?"

I said in aggressive voice. "Why were you talking to that guy you don't know, his intensions are never correct. He is flirtatious.

She was staring me weirdly & might have smelled jealousy in me. She laughed &said, "So what if I talked to some other guy. He asked about the exams only, nothing else. Why are you getting hyper?

I said, "Whatever, you don't know Aaliya, he is not a good guy. It's not good to stand beside such a boy & have a word with him." My pitch was getting more aggressive.

She said, "Ok ... Ok." calm down. I am sorry. Now onwards I will not talk to him, fine.

I took a deep breathe to calm down myself & the thought why I got so hyper. Can't she even talk to a guy for some work? We are just good friends. I can't bind her whom to talk & whom not to. I realised that I over reacted on that such a stupid thing. The classes were going she was sitting beside me. From past 3 hours she hasn't spoken a single word. I thought she might have felt bad the way a scolded her. I tore out a piece of paper from the back of my notebook & wrote on that

☹ "I am sorry for that stupid & idiotic behaviour I did with you in the morning. I behaved very badly. Please don't mind." ☹

I folded that paper & dragged it towards her. She saw that paper & unfolded it. She read that & smiled. She wrote on the other side of that paper.

It's Ok ☺

I smiled & took a sigh of relief. She hasn't taken it otherwise. In evening I told Samarth about that incident. He was laughing at me & said. "I am telling you, you like her. A pinch of possessiveness has developed in you for her. You wish that no other boy should talk to her. In front of you, she may not talk but what if she talks on phone. Maybe she is already having a boyfriend.

I shouted at him after hearing this. "How could you say this?" He then pointed towards the balcony from where, we can see Aaliya roaming in balcony & talking on phone and that scene burnt my ass. But I controlled myself.

I said to Samarth, "May be she is talking to any of her cousin or any friend."

Samarth said, "My dear Aaru, I am observing her like this since very first day. Every day she stands in the balcony of her room & talks on phone for almost an hour.

I got depressed after hearing this. I started observing her for the next 10 days Yes, she used to talk on phone every night & yes almost for an hour & half. I was getting nothing what to do? Should I ask her about this? How will she react? This is a personal question.

I left the thought of asking her about this and for the next 10 months me & Samarth argue to have a debate and the topic was Whether I am in love with Aaliya or not? He was in favour & I was in against. In these 10 months, I & Aaliya became very close friends we used to share secrets. Whenever I say to her that I am missing my Mom, she used to pamper a lot. We used to call each other Babe; we do late night chatting on phone, chit chatting in class room. There was no end to our talks. Meanwhile a year was over. Our first year of BBA was over. We now entered to the second year. After a year, college announced vacations. We all were going to our home. She was leaving for Nagpur & me for Bangalore. I reached Bangalore after 2 days I messaged Aaliya. "I reached home."

I got no reply from her. I reached home & met Bhaiya Bhabhi. Rohan was expecting some gifts from me. I brought few chocolates for him. Bhabhi said me, "Aaru, go & get fresh. I serve dinner for you." I went for shower I was too tired. And that chilled water was removing my tiredness. Under the shower I was thinking about Aaliya only. I was missing her. Her smile, her cute nose, her glistening eyes, her red shaded hair .... "How will I survive without her for 20 days? I got to know, these 20 days will be like hell for me. I came out of washroom and went out for dinner. Bhabhi prepared all my favourite dishes. I enjoyed my dinner a lot. The mess food has destroyed the taste of my mouth. I ate lots of onions that day. I ate a lot that my stomach was about to burst. I finished my dinner Bhaiya then asked me about college, I gave him my annual report of First year. He was satisfied & told me to keep it up. "Haashh". I was on the marks of Bhaiya, as I was too tired. I jumped on my bed & checked my phone. No reply from Aaliya I got bit upset & closed my eyes. Don't know when fell asleep. In the morning, when I woke up I saw 3 missed calls. Those were from Aaliya she called me at 1 a.m. late night. But I was sleeping. One message was also there.

"Sorry I couldn't reply at that time. I was busy with Mom."

I read that & kept phone again on bed, her one message in the morning was enough to make my day Bhabhi called me for morning tea. I said, "Yes coming Bhabhi."

I went to washroom to brush my teeth & wash my face. I came out of the room & sat on the chair. Bhaiya & Rohan were having their breakfast. Bhaiya has to leave for office & Rohan has to go to school. Only I & Bhabhi were there in home & she was usually busy in kitchen works. I took bath & then had breakfast. After that I was having no work to do. I opened my laptop. Logged in face book and guess what I had found "Aaliya Online" A green dot beside her name. There was no limit of my excitement. But the limit that crossed was of my bad luck. As soon as I typed "Hi", she went offline. Huh. I logged out immediately I was seeing her pictures in my laptop. Her smiling pictures, her angry pictures, picture of her glittering eyes her cute nose and as usual I was smiling like an idiot whenever I think about her, a smile glows on my face, and at that time Bhabhi caught me smiling alone in my room. She knocked on the door & asked. "What has happened Arhaan?"

I was blank, speechless at that time. Smile was furrrr at that time. I said, "Nothing"

She said "Oh. Then why are you smiling, sitting alone in room. Come on tell me what's the matter? I can easily read your face."

I said, "Nothing Bhabhi, its nothing like that.

She said, "You got a girlfriend? Come on say, who is she?

Now I started blushing my cheeks were red & she pinched my cheeks & said, come on say.

I said, "First promise, you won't tell anything to Bhaiya."

She promised that. I explained her "Actually she studies with me in my class. Her name is Aaliya. She is very sweet girl. So beautiful I like her a lot. We both are very good friends. But I haven't expressed my feeling to her yet. And I don't wanna tell her even.

Bhabhi asked. "Why?"

I said, "We both are very good friends and we spent almost whole day together. If she doesn't like my way of expressing my feelings, then she might break our friendship. I don't know how I will survive then.

Bhabhi was smiling by looking at my idiotic blushing face. She laughed & said, "Ok. Good I would like to see her.

I showed all the pictures of Aaliya to Bhabhi in my laptop. Bhabhi said in a teasing way." Hmm. She is ok ok types.

I said, "What ok ok, she is the only one for me." Bhabhi again laughed & said, "Ya ya she is really so pretty. You will make a good pair." I smiled & said "Thanks. ☺

The days without her were passing badly. Though we used to chat & talk on phone every night, but I wanna see her. I thought to ask her for few more pictures of her, and then I left this thought. Every night we talk on phone for almost 1 hour and every night after talking to her, I keep smiling. Every night I try to sleep, but sleep was far away from my eyes. I dream about Aaliya with my eyes open. Her face, with her most killing smile, her united silky hair, all this was roaming all around my eyes. I wish I could catch her in my dreams & hug her tightly, I wanna show her my intense love I was feeling a kind of sweet fragrance all around when I do fantasy about her.

I heard the doorbell I then woke out from my past I opened the door. It was laundry man. My head was busting. I was not willing to prepare any kind of food for myself. And also was not willing to go out and have a lunch outside alone. But still I was hungry. So I went to a nearby restaurant to have something. As I entered I heard somebody calling my name "Arhaan" I looked around. It was Samarth. He called me to join him. Actually, Samarth & Naina came there for their Sunday date. And they called me to join their date I was having no option. I joined them & had lunch with them. I & Samarth paid half of the bill. We left the restaurant, I came home back. Don't know but why she is not leaving my mind. With each passing day, just one question, where is she?

I rested myself on couch, turned on the T.V. nothing interesting. Turn it off. I again turned on the TV of my past.

Our vacations were over & I saw her after a month. I was already in the class & she was approaching me to our seat.

8

I said "Hi". She looked at me & smiled. Oh God ... Yes, her that killing smile, which I was missing a lot. I removed my bag from the seat & made place for her to sit. She said beside me & asked. "So how was the vacation?"

I said, "It was boring. Bhaiya couldn't get leave from office, so he was unable to go out for a family trip. And it's impossible to go alone for an enjoyable trip. She said, "Ya true." At the same time, Sir came to the class disturbing me in my important conversation.

That day was normal as all the other days. But for me, days were not normal. Every day I experience something extra-ordinary in me. The mornings were much brighter & the nights were much colder & beautiful I give emphasis on Samarth's words. He was right, I am in Love. But still, I wanna give some more time to myself. Days were passing, & with everyday which was passing, my feelings were increasing. Every night we use to stand in balcony, looking each other from a far distance & talking on phone. Every morning, the first face I see was of her in the balcony. That balcony of my hostel room was like heaven for me. I was getting more & more close to her. She now started ruling my dream, my smiles, my words, my mood. My everything varies according to her only. This feeling I never experienced, new thoughts, a new way of thinking, a new style of living. It was everything new & every new thing was beautiful. The air was fresh & fragranced every time.

Something was there all around. But don't know what, these symptoms were strange but they were making me sick in this beautiful world. These things were making me realise that there is something wrong with me. Not wrong in fact something good in about to happen with me.

Love changes you. You're becoming the person you never thought you could be. You're changing either for bad or good.

One day I was observing Aaliya in garden with her friends. All girls were sitting there in a group & were discussing something. I was little far from that place, but was able to hear their gossips I was observing her each & every action, her smile her laughs, her hair, which shows putting in the back of her ear again& again. Here beautifully created hands, fingers, and nails, everything. That charm on her face always overrides my sense. She makes me senseless.

Suddenly my soul shouted at me, "Mr Arhaan Kashyap. You are in love with Aaliya ..."

My mouth shouted more loudly, "No". My No was so loud that those girls heard that. They all gave me a weird look. I left that place in embarrassment. That night I couldn't sleep. The only question was coming in my mind. Am I really in love with Aaliya? Does she also feel the same as I feel for her? Should

I tell her about all this? What I am experiencing from past so many months? Will she accept this? Will this lead to a good relationship or she will break our good friendship then how will I survive without her? My affection for her has increased to that level, that now I cannot live without her. What should I do? I was getting nothing. The whole night passed in the puzzles of these questions. Finally in the morning 4 am I decided to express my feelings to her on upcoming Valentine's Day. Exactly one month later. Now I was feeling sleep, so I closed my eyes. I woke up at 8 am. Samarth was already gone for his classes. I got ready for my classes. I was moving towards the lecture hall, suddenly Aaliya called me from back. I turned around; she said "Good morning".

Her smile… I was about to faint. But controlled myself I replied "Ya good morning". She asked "Why haven't you come for breakfast today? Are you alright?

I said, "Ya, Ya I am fine. I woke up late, so that's why, couldn't come for breakfast."

She said "Oh I thought if you won't come today for class, what I will do alone for the whole day."

I laughed and we entered the class.

She loves my company. Great!!

As usual we sat together and the lecture was going on and my favourite scene too. The wind from window was playing with her hair. I just love it when she keeps her hair at the back of ear again a gust of wind make them come in front again. This was disturbing her and was entertaining me. I wish I could hold her hair all the time so that she won't get disturbed.

9

For the next 1 month, every night I wrote so many letters I could give her. I tried hard to write my exact feelings in words, but that seems to be very difficult task. Every night I waste hundreds of papers and each of them was useless. Samarth also tried to help me in this, but was of no use. Now just one week was left. In this one week, I came to know that her friends used to tease her with my name. That means she talks about me with them. It means something was there in her mind too. But, either she likes me, that's why her friends used to tease she or, she don't like me at all, that's why her friend used to tease her. This was the signal, to be happy and even to get panic too. Still I didn't lose hope, and finally at the night of 12th Feb I wrote my exact feelings in words. That letter which I can give to her.

Hey Aaliya,

Please. Don't mind after reading this.

How can I ever arrange my words to say? How special you are to me.

You are theme of my Life. You are the Beloved Princess.

You are my love. You are in my memories.

You are in my happiness. You are in my all Acceptances.

Every single beat of my heart is just for you.

Every breathe I inhale is just for you honey.

I live for you and I will die for you.

I laugh and cry for you. All this is because

I want to do something special for you!

Every day that goes by, it seems like I discover something new about you to love. It's incredible to me how one person can make such a big difference in my life. You touched me in a way name else ever has and gave me so many reasons to love you. I never felt a love like this before. It's a love like no other. Something I have always hoped for.

A love with friendship, humour and heart; a bond so strong, it would never part; a love that makes me smile; a love that is joyful without any fear; a love that is beautiful, from the inside out; a love with no tears, pain or doubt; a love with Soul, so tender and True; a love that I have found, only in you.

My feelings are truly pure for you. If you accept my proposal I will be the luckiest person of this world. I am not forcing you for anything; it's all up to you to decide how to respond. Even if you say NO, I promise, I will never ask or say anything to you in future regarding this. We will be friends as we are. Hope you will understand the depth of my feelings and will reply with a positive answer.

Yours and Only Yours

Arhaan

Finally this was what all I could articulate. I folded that letter and kept in book. The next morning, on 13th February; I was getting ready for the college Samarth said "Best of Luck dude. Don't take tension. She will say yes only"

I smiled and said "Ya I hope that too". *Crossed my fingers*

I came to college with the letter in my bag. The day for all was normal but for me it was extra-ordinary.

My legs were shivering while entering in the class. I entered and was searching for her. She was not there anywhere in the class. I got tensed; she will attend lectures today or not. I thought to message her, but then left this thought. I found a seat and sat on that waiting for her. Sir has already started the lecture, but there was no sign of her entry in the class. Finally, she came 15 minutes late. Asked sir to come in and was approaching upwards. She was searching me there and I raised my hand to call her. She smile and approached me. She came there and sat beside me. She was breathing hard. I offered her some water, she drank and relaxed herself. I asked "Why you have come so late today?"

She said "I got up late. Actually I slept late last night, was completing the assignment.

In my mind Assignment Oh Fish!! **"The Assignment"** In writing that letter for Aaliya, I forgot to do assignment of Finance Marketing. Now what to do, where to go?

I asked her about her assignment, the work was of 35 pages, impossible to do this much work in an hour. Aaliya asked about my assignment. I said "I forgot"

She was shocked "How can you forget such an important assignment at your room."

I gave weird look to her & she then said, "Don't tell me you forgot to even do it."

My eyes were showing guilt. She was about to scold me, but then she realised that we are in class. No other option left. I have to confront the punishment. The assignment has to be submitted in the next lecture. A terror was flowing in my blood, Aaliya could see me tensed face & said, "Don't worry; no serious action will be taken for this."

The bell rang; yes that 1 hour was over. Mehta Sir entered the room & asked everyone to submit the assignment. Aaliya stood up & went in front to submit. I followed her.

Everybody was keeping their assignment & was leaving but I was still standing there. Aaliya was standing beside me. Sir asked me, "yes, Arhaan, where's your assignment?"

I said, Sir actually I forgot to do this. I am sorry Sir." He shouted at me." What do you mean you forgot to do? I don't want any excuse. Submit it now or get suspended for 2 days. **"Suspension and that too of 2 days"** I looked at Aaliya who clearly said. **"No serious action will be taken."** Is suspension of 2 days not a serious action?

Sir continued. "Not only suspension of 2 days you have to do your assignment 5 times in your own hand writing." He shouted too loud that everybody in class heard that. My mind said, 'come on this man is insulting you in front of the whole class, hit him on his face." But heart said, "No it's your mistake. You forgot this in writing letter for Aaliya. You have to endure all this. Don't make issues just do what he says.

I said, "Ok Sir" & left the class. I went outside the canteen. I was so tensed that I wished to smoke to calm down myself. I saw few guys smoking so I wished to do same. Though I never smoked before, but that day I bought a packet of cigarette & took out one from it. I put it in between of my lips & lit it. And yes, I was perfect in smoking I haven't coughed for once. I was smoking, and Samarth called me from back & sat beside me. He was shocked to see me smoking. Samarth used to smoke, but I never tried. He gave me a pat & said, "Good dude, keep it up." He asked one cigarette for himself. Now we both were smoking I told Samarth about my suspension. He was laughing hard at my condition but afterwards he consoled me. After 2 hours, Aaliya called me "Where are you Arhaan?

You went back to your room? I said, "No, I am in canteen you come here." She said, "Ok coming in 10 minutes

Samarth asked, "You gave letter to her?". Shit I forgot to do even that. I said "No." He said, "Then when will you give, on next Valentine's Day?"

Till then Aaliya came there. Her roommate was also there with her. I introduced them with Samarth, and Aaliya introduced her roommate Naina to us. Aaliya asked me "You had something?" I said, "No, not in mood to eat something. It's impossible to do that assignment 5 times. In just 2 days. 35 x 5 = 175 pages, almost a book. My head was rotating. She said, "Calm down Arhaan. You do it for 3 times & I will help you. I will do it 2 times for you." Is that Ok?" I wish I could hug her for this, but just managed to say thanks in words. She smiled & I was bowled again. She said, "Now, go & bring something to eat for all of us. I said, "Samarth come, "But he didn't respond. I looked at him." Oh God, What a scene? Naina & Samarth were staring into each other's eyes. What the hell? What's this going on? Aaliya was laughing looking at them & said "Don't you know about their love story." I was shocked "Love Story of Samarth" started when. He never told me about this. How, when where it started" Aaliya said, "Ask your friend only. Let's go from here & get them drown into each other's eyes." I was about to kill Samarth for this But left that thought for a while. I & Aaliya bought few snacks & coke for both of us. Aaliya was getting a call. It was from her dad. She stood up & went bit side to talk. I was staring her. Her red shaded hair was flowing softly in air & suddenly my mind stroked about the letter. I took it out from my bag & keep it in her bag while she was still on phone. I was done with my work & she came after 15 minutes. We then paid the bill & she gave me her assignment file so that I can complete that easily. She said, "Bye! will miss you in class for 2 days." This made me smile. I said, "Ya ya see you at dinner." We then proceeded towards our hostels. I decided to tell her about that letter after dinner. I hope till then she doesn't see her bag. I was moving towards my hostel with ear phones in my ear. The sweet lyrics were playing.

"Din bhar kare baate hum, phir bi lage, baate adhuri aaj kal.

Mann ki dehlizo pe koi aayena, bas tum zaroori aajkal."

Abra me hu, tu aasma hai, pas hai tu, par kaha hai

Zidd meri tu nahi, meri aadat hai tu

I love uuuu.....

And throughout the song I was feeling heaven all around. Love is the most beautiful feeling in the world. And I am experiencing this. And I pray that Aaliya too feels the same I reached my room & I was still smiling. I went in the balcony. She was there in her balcony, but was on phone with someone. It was still a mystery that with whom she talks for hours in the balcony. I was staring at her. Talking on phone, she moved in. ☹

I too came inside & relaxed on my bed. As I haven't slept for the whole night, I fell asleep in a sound sleep. I heard Samarth calling me. "Arhaan get up, it's dinner time." I was drowsy so I turned myself & didn't respond to him. I again feel asleep. I suddenly woke up after few minutes. I checked my watch I was 8.30 pm. then checked my phone there were 5 missed calls & 2 messages from Aaliya. I opened the message.

Message 1 "Where are you? Don't you wanna come for dinner?"

Message 2 "Come soon. I am waiting for you."

I rushed towards the mess without even washing my face & eyes properly. Thank god, the mess was not closed yet and she was inside waiting for me. I sat beside her & we were now having our dinner. She looked at me. You were sleeping." I said, "Ya, how you came to know?" She said, "Your face is saying that you are still in half sleep. I laughed & then after few minutes we were finished with our dinner.

Samarth came to me & said, "Oh you woke up?" I said, "Ya and you don't talk me. I will see you in room."

He laughed & said, "Ok, shall I wait for you or you will come afterwards?"

I said, "You go I will come later."

After that I & Aaliya were having a walk in the lawn between the hostels.

I said, "I haven't slept for the whole night that's why I was little sleepy. She said, "Why so" Haven't slept for the whole night & still haven't done the assignment. What were you doing then?

I said, "Actually I was writing letter for you. Not in the last night but from past one month.

She was shocked. I continued "The letter is in your bag just go & read that & tell me about that soon.

She asked me, "What are the contents of that letter?"

I said, "Please read it yourself."

She said, "Ok I will see Bye."

I said, "Bye" We both again went towards our respective hostels. I reached my room. My heart was beating very fast. I was shivering. I was feeling a weird kind of pressure inside me. It was like; I will burst in few minutes. I was feeling cold, but at the same time there were few drops of sweat also on my forehead. I was scared of losing her now.

Samarth was in washroom. He saw me in such a stressed state & asked. "What happened?" I said, "I told her about the letter. She will read that tonight."

I then remembered to ask him about Naina. I asked "You tell me first, what's going on between you & Naina? He laughed & said, "Nothing dude." I said, in anger "Oh Nothing, then what were you doing in canteen & why Aaliya said that a Love story is going between you & Naina.

He was laughing loud & started his explanation. "Did you not know it? Few months back, one wrong number was disturbing me again and again." I said "Ya, who was that?"

Samarth said "That was Naina only". We became friends on the phone, and then came to know that we are in same college and then friendship changed to close friendship and now.

I said "But why haven't you told me about this earlier?" He said "Because I was not serious with her, but now I seriously wanna get serious with her and she too wishes the same."

I said "Ok", that's good for both of you, but what about me. He consoled me "Don't worry, she will say yes only. There's no reason for her to say no.

Samarth slept, but sleep was far away from my eyes. I thought to message Aaliya. I took my phone and message her.

"You read that letter".

An instant reply, "Yes, I read".

I don't know what she was feeling at that time, but the message was sounding bit rude. Don't know why. I couldn't message her further. I kept my phone down and started the work of assignment. The night was passing, the time was slow.

I was in tension, my blood pressure was low. In morning, I woke up at 9 am. The college has started. But what I have to do with that I was suspended. I checked my phone. There was a message from Aaliya "Meet me after dinner tonight". I sensed something rude in that. I am gone. She is going to break friendship. No, I couldn't wait till evening. But I cannot say anything to her. I replied "Ok, Happy Valentine's Day".

She replied after 10 minutes: "Same to you ☺".

I went to mess for breakfast and came back soon and started doing my assignment. The anxiousness of last night made me to write so fast. That unbelievably I completed my assignment 3 times.

10

This time I came out of my past with again a door bell. All the girls came to my home Naina, Rumana and Sarah "Hi Arhaan." They all said together as I opened the gate. It was evening 7:30pm. I said, "Hi, you all here, together. What's the matter?"

They all came inside and comfortably sat on the couches I too sat. Naina said "Actually Arhaan your bhabhi called me one hour back and told me to ask you something ". I said, "Oh really what to ask tell?"

She told me to find a perfect girl for you to whom you can marry, I laughed and said, "You think I am going to support you in this?"

Rumana said "Arhaan your bhaiya and bhabhi are serious this time. They want you to forget Aaliya and restart your life". I got bit serious and said, "NO that's impossible how can I forget Aaliya, no one can replace her in my heart. You all know from last 3 days, she is clicking my mind again and again. In past 2 years I never thought this much about her as much as I am thinking about her now a days. I tried hard to get her back but she never responded to me. I still don't know what wrong happened with her that she even broke our engagement and left me alone forever. I just want to know my mistake; just a genuine reason for our breakup. The feeling to get her back kills me from inside every day. This separation is unbearable for me. But I am helpless. There's nothing in my hands. I stopped saying and tears rolled down from my eyes. Naina wiped them and said," I know how much you love her. I saw you both together, I felt the love between you two, but just give emphasis on your mind then think how long you want to wait for her. It's too late, she won't come back now."

Sarah said, "This time now at least think about your family. They also love you. Don't you respect them? You will deny them just for a girl who left you in these days when you needed her most.

Sarah was right. She left me when I needed her the most. My head was giddy. All girls were trying to convince me to get married soon. They too are about to get married soon even Naina and Samarth were getting married next month. They all gave me lectures for almost 2 hours. I assured them that I'll get married soon give some more time to me. They all agreed and left. I too then prepared a cup of tea for myself in one hand a cup of tea and in another hand a cigarette. My mind again went in flashback. The day when I proposed her and was waiting for 14th February, it was announced in the college that in the evening there will be celebration for Valentine's eve and dress code for boys was black and for girls was red. It was so much of noise, so much of crowd and I was searching for Aaliya. I was waiting for her reply. Samarth said, "Hey Arhaan there is a demand for your song in this beautiful evening" and I said "No dude, I don't wanna sing"

He said, "Come on dude, sing a romantic song. Impress her with your song. Here's your guitar, go ahead." Meanwhile I thought that's a good idea to impress her more.

In that crowd I saw her coming in red shirt and black jeans and she was looking so stunning. She came and stood far away from me but just in front of my eyes. Then I played the strings of guitar.

11

I looked into her eyes and started my song.

"Pehli nazar me kesa jaadu kar diya.

Tera bann betha hai mera jiya..

Aaj ki raat dil ki ye baat..

Kehke rahunga tujse..

Haa kar tu ya naa keh de

Izhaar toh kar mujse.."

There were clapping all around, Aaliya was clapping too. But all I need was the answer YES or NO. I wanna talk to her but how, in this crowd so I messaged her "Meet me outside the mess I am waiting". She replied "Sorry I can't come. We will meet later".

Seeing her reply I was heartbroken now it was confirmed it was a no and our friendship is over. She refused to talk to me, to meet me, everything is over. **"THE END"** I got disappointed and went to my room I received one message from Aaliya "check your mail"

Oh God! She replied. My heart was beating fast. I don't have guts to open her mail. I don't want to read that. I told Samarth that she replied through mail. He consoled me and encouraged me to open her mail. I finally opened that and it was written:

"Hey Arhaan, I read your letter, very well written glad to know that you have such a pure feelings for me. Thank you so much for that. You are my very special friend. But you might get disappointed that those pure feeling hasn't developed in me yet. I accept that I like you, I do care for you; I respect your feelings but haven't experienced the love. No doubt, I enjoy your company. I find myself incomplete without you but please give me some time to answer you properly. I wanna assure myself that even I am in love with you and for that you have to wait. I really don't wanna hurt your feelings but you also try to understand me. I really respect your love for me I am really touched with your beautiful words that you wrote for me. Thanks once again, hope you won't feel bad. Take care"

I really didn't get disappointed if she respects my love then I must also respect her reply. I took my phone and messaged her

"Hey Aaliya read your mail, glad to know that you respect my feelings thank you so much for that, no issues take your time I promise won't say anything regarding this until you wish"

She replied after 5 minutes "Thanks and thanks for that song. You have never told about your this recreation" I replied, "Ya, I saved my talent for this day only" she replied "Oh but really you sing so well, so clear, so soft now I am fan of your singing"

I replied "thank you." She said "Have you completed you assignment?" I replied "Ya, I did for 3 times. Tomorrow I will complete that for 2 more times you don't worry" She replied "Hmm Okays good night." I replied "good night sweet dreams"

I then slept and woke up at 9 am got fresh and again sat to do my assignment 70 pages work more. I completed the assignment for the 4th time and went for bath. After that I went out to city, took the bus from the main road in front of my college, went to market and bought my daily use things soap, toothpaste, shaving gel, comb etc. I returned back to hostel at 4 pm.

I checked my phone no calls, no messages. I went to balcony, Aaliya was there too in her balcony she was there with Naina they both were talking I messaged her, "hi look here."

She read message and looked at me and waved her hand at me with a big smile. I too waved my hand. She asked with sign language "Have you completed assignment?" I too replied in an analogical language "No, need to do one more time" She did action of OK and waved bye.

I too waved bye and came in. Samarth too came in room. He was in mood of teasing me he said "dude, you got trolled."

I said "How trolled?" Giving a weird look he said "You wrote a long love letter, sang a romantic song, still she hasn't got impressed."

We both laughed and then I sat for doing my assignment for one more time and submitted that next day. Days were passing as usual and by each passing day my love and respect for her was increasing.

12

March came, and so do exams, month of Aaliya's Birthday, **very special date, 15ᵗʰ March.** Our exams started on 1st March & were over on 13th March. We all did our best. Now our 2nd year of BBA was complete. We all were again going home for vacations. Everybody will leave hostel before 15. I asked Aaliya when she is leaving for home. She said 16th March. Great! We can celebrate her birthday together. I thought to do something special for her. But no, she will take in another way. Again I thought no. I will do lots of things for her but merely as a good friend. I will never let her feel my love till she allows me to do so.

"When you love someone, don't expect them to love you as much as you do. But love them so much that they don't want to be loved by anyone else but you."

I went to the market along with Naina & Samarth to buy gifts for her. She loves all girlish things. Soft toys, dresses, sandals, ear rings, chocolates, flower etc. etc.

First of all we bought a chocolate cake. Then we went to gift shop & bought a soft toy of a dolphin and a nice white top for her. A pack of chocolates & a bunch of red roses & a birthday card shopping was done. She was calling me & Naina repeatedly because we left her alone in the hostel. We reached back to the hostel. All gifts were with Naina. I told her to hide somewhere and I called Aaliya in the lawn. She was very angry & I was engaged in making her calm down. In this time, Naina went upstairs to their room & hide all those gifts in the room. Naina indicated us from the balcony. Then I said bye to Aaliya & come back to my room. I & Samarth got fresh & then we went for dinner. After dinner we all four sat in common lawn & watched T.V, till 10 pm. After that we said good night to each other & came to our respective rooms. After roaming whole day in market I was very tired. I couldn't keep my eyes open. But I have to wake up till 12am. I wanna wish her first I kept my eyes open till 11.30. Now I couldn't walk any more so I fell down on my bed. Finally my watch displayed 11.55. I called her, Ring was going. She picked up after a while, a soft hello from her side. I sang happy birthday song for her. After I finished my song, she said, "Oh, How sweet of you Arhaan! …. Thank you so much."

I said, "Your welcome, come to the balcony. I wanna see you. She said. "Ok, wait for a minute. I am coming."

She came to the balcony, how beautiful she was looking in the full moon night! The brightness of moon was falling on her face as a spot light. Her face was shining in that Moonlight. I said to her, "There are few surprises for you in your room. You have a task to find these surprises in just 15 minutes, And for these 15 minutes, you cannot keep the phone down. She said "Oh surprises. Really…?"

I said "Ya go and seek them. Your time starts now." She said in hurry, "Yeah, Ok" & she went in.

She said, "Let me search under pillow ....Oh, there's a birthday card. I got one.

I laughed & said, "Yeah, but still 3 more ...."

She then said, "Let me open my wardrobe. Oh!! A dolphin, it's so cute ..."

I said, "Search more in your wardrobe......."

She searched & found chocolate box & said." Awww.. Chocolates. I love them."

This all was making me happy & probably her too.

She asked, "Now where??

I said, "You can't even think about that place?"

She said, What? Bathroom? Is that a place to hide a surprise gift?"

I laughed & said just go & see it.

She went in, "I couldn't find anything in bathroom."

I said, "See at the back of the door."

She said, "Oh my god it's so beautiful. Such a pretty top ...Thank you so much."

I was feeling a great joy inside me.

She continued, "You have really made my birthday special."

She came in balcony & gave a flying kiss to me. I immediately caught that. She laughed & said, "Now can I go?"

I said, "No I need a return gift from you ...."

She said, "Oh a return gift. Say what you want?"

I said, "I need a name by which, only you can call me, nobody else.

She said, "Oh another task, "Ok", I will give, but give me some time.

I said, "Ok", Take your time. Now I am putting down the phone. I'm very tired.

She said, "Ok", Bye & thank you so much once again.

She waved her hand from balcony cut the phone. I did the same & we two went in our rooms. I lay on my bed & was fantasising about her. I then received a message from her. "Why you did so much for me?"

I replied, "Because, you are a very special friend of mine." ☺

She again messaged, "You love me a lot no?"

I was shocked by this message, but replied "Ya, a lot ...." ☺

I thought she is going to accept my proposal tonight. But no she messaged, "I thought a name for you."

I asked, "What?"

She replied, **"My jhallah wallah aashiq."**

I busted out in laughter then controlled myself & replied to her. Oh, **"My jallah wallah aashiq."** That's cool. I liked it. Thank you.

She replied, "☺Now please sleep I'm also very tired."

I replied, "Ya sleep. Good Night Sweet dreams.

The beautiful morning of 15th March, the season of spring, sunrays entered in my room & they woke me up. The morning was so fresh & yes my heart was so happy & I was so excited. The air was breezing with fragrance. Even the birds were chirping & singing to wish Aaliya. Hmm for the first time, I was not feeling lazy in the Sunday morning. I went for shower. Even the water of shower was having essence, cold. Everything was beautiful. As if the flowers were showering on me. It was her birthday, but why I am so happy. May be, she is the one who is so close to me, that's why, I was very eager to see her. I knew, today she will be looking the most beautiful girl of this world.

I got ready & went down stairs with Samarth towards the mess. Naina was already there preparing a small party for Aaliya. She decorated a table & kept the cake on that. I asked Naina about Aaliya. She said, "She is about to come......."

We all gathered around the table. She came, I saw her on the entrance. She was looking WOW, in the white cocktail dress. Her untied red shaded hair was falling on her face. She was wearing simple, but was looking super awesome in white. Her fair complexion was generating brightness all around. I was just staring her. This beauty was approaching towards us. We all wished her & then she stood between us. She blew the candles & we all clapped. The first piece of cake she offered me. That made me feel special, I took half from that & offered her half. After that we all went out of hostel for celebration.

The whole day we enjoyed in Kankaria Lake. We had lunch there, went for boating, rides. Even we went to zoo, watched so many animals, the birds, they were so beautiful. Many different coloured parrots & love birds. We too went for a ride in hot air balloon. Naina & Aaliya were screaming as it was going up. Aaliya held my hand very tightly. I was just seeing her, she was enjoying & getting scared at the same time. We all enjoying a lot there for the whole day clicked so many pictures. After having dinner we went to the disc. We danced a lot there. She was so happy & her happiness was transferring in me. At 10 pm we came out of disc, we were getting late to go back the hostel. We hired a taxi from Ambawadi & returned back to hostel 10.30 p.m. Samarth & Naina were busy in their own. Aaliya said to me, "Arhaan, thank you so much for making my birthday memorable, the most memorable day of my life." I smiled & then suddenly she hugged me. A current passed through my whole body, I skipped my heartbeat with her touch. She was hugging tightly and then moved back. We both were speechless. I said, "Ok, its ok, let's leave Goodnight."

She said, "Ya Bye Good Night."

We then waved and turned. Samarth & Naina were still standing there. Samarth said, "Yo Dude, she hugged you, and that too, so tightly?"

I was blushing. Naina said, "He deserves that Samarth."

I laughed & said to Samarth, "Shall we move towards our room or you both wanna talk more??"

Samarth said, "You turn around for a while."

I said, "You do your romance I am going in room."

I then moved out from there & they both continued their romance.

While I was on my way room I received message from Aaliya "Thank you so much my jhallah wallah aashiq."

Come soon in balcony I'm waiting for you ...."

Reading this, I ran towards my room opened the door & quickly went to the balcony. She was already there, waiting for me. I messaged her. "Yes say, here I am."

She again gave a flying kiss to me & yes I caught that too. The whole night we were in balcony chatting with each other on phone. We went inside our room at 3.30 a.m. The next morning we all were leaving for our homes. She left for Nasik & me for Bangalore. At that time of leaving I wished I could get her hug for one more time, so that I can survive for 3 months without her. But ....

All the time in train, I was thinking about her. I couldn't call or message her due to roaming. The whole way I slept & ate. Nothing else I could do. I reached Bangalore after 30 hours of travel; again Bhaiya asked my annual report of II year. I was on his marks again. He was happy and this time he got leave too from office. He has already booked ticket for our vacations in Goa.....

Wow, me, Bhaiya, Bhabhi & Rohan were going Goa. I was so excited. I messaged Aaliya that I am going Goa in vacation.

She replied, "Great, I am going Mumbai.

I asked: Why Mumbai? Why don't you also come to Goa?

She replied, "Haha Nice idea but tickets are booked."

I replied ☹ Oh

She replied "Aww you are completely a dramebaaz.."

I replied "Dramebaaz... LOL, how??

She replied, "Haha ☺some other day. I am little busy now, will talk to you later Bye."

I replied, "Ohk ☺Bye."

We used to chat and talk on phone for hours daily. I went Goa with my family, enjoyed a lot there but couldn't contact Aaliya for these 15 days when I was in Goa.

13

It was morning, the whole evening, the whole night, sitting on couch, smoking, I was in my past. I stood up and looked myself in mirror. What I have made myself? Really, a complete insane and that I don't wanna be. I took bath and got ready for office. Reached office and had breakfast, I got notice from CEO that there is a meeting at 11:30 am regarding the new constructions. I checked my watch; it was 10:45 am 45 minutes more to prepare my data. Within 30 minutes, I was done with my work and reached the conference hall for meeting. Everybody reached there and meeting started. The M.D. was explaining something blah blah. But I was still lost. He pointed me Mr Kashyap; please proceed with your report. I stood up and started with my report, explained each point thoroughly and finished with 25 min. After that a general discussion held and meeting was over. I came out of conference hall at 1:30 pm. It was lunch time I went to canteen to have my lunch. The lunch was tasteless that day. I left it and came back to my room. I sat on my chair Aaliya, Aaliya and Aaliya was ruling my mind. I don't know why? I took out our pic from the drawer; saw it, the pic, 4 years back on my birthday, when we returned back to college after the vacation of II year. We were about to start our new session on 16 July as it was Monday. We all reached hostel on 14 July itself. Till afternoon everyone was there and we all met in the mess during our lunch. Aah, saw Aaliya after a month, I was about to fell down but Samarth held me. She smiled and said 'Hi', I was about to fell down again, this time, Naina held me. She smiled again & I replied. "How are you?" She said, I am fine, how's you? I am fine too, come let's have lunch. We all four sat on one bench with our lunch; Samarth & Naina usually have their meals in one plate only. I & Aaliya were obviously having separate plates. We all were tired to go to our rooms to take rest. Next day was my birthday. In evening I was chatting with Aaliya standing in balcony. We again met at dinner. Samarth asked me, "What's your plan for tomorrow? Where we are going to celebrate? I said, "Nowhere", I don't have that much money to spend on a party. If we all contribute then it won't be a party a simple get together. Useless even I myself don't wanna celebrate.

Samarth sensed the sadness inside me. He left that place with Naina. Now me Aaliya were there. She came closer & kept her hand on my shoulder & said, "You are sounding upset. What happened? You can share with me, if you want".

I looked at her. Some tears were there in my eyes & I said, "Actually I was missing mom & dad a lot. Since they passed no one celebrated any occasion. She wiped my tear & said, "But how long you will do this. Tomorrow is your birthday if your parents see you like this; they will also feel bad, their souls will in ache. For the peace of their soul at least stay happy. Don't weep like this. I hugged her & she pampered me & made me calm down, I moved back. She wiped my tears and I smiled at her. It was 9.30 pm. She said, "Let's go now it's too late. We stood up said, "Good Night" & proceeded towards our room. Samarth met me on the way. We went together and relaxed on bed. Opened my laptop & started playing angry bird with headphones in my ear. At 11.45 p.m., 15 min. before my birthday, I received a message. It was from Aaliya. It was written.

Open your Gmail there's something for you there."

I replied, "What's there?"

She replied, "See by yourself. It's a surprise for you.

I opened my Gmail in excitement & logged in. It was taking time to get load. It was killing me; I couldn't wait to see what she has sent. Finally it opened inbox. There was a mail from Aaliya Juneja. I clicked on it. And again it was loading ....

Finally it opened. There was a long letter.

Suddenly my phone rang. I came out of my past & saw my phone. It was Naina calling I said, "Hello." She said "Hey Arhaan" Her voice was lucidly telling that she was very happy. I asked, "What happened? You seem to be very happy. "Yes come to Faizan's house." It's urgent. She said, "Don't ask questions just come fast." I said, "Ok", I am coming. I kept the phone & moved out of the office. Drove & reached Faizan's house.

Everybody was there Samarth happily received me & said, "Come dude, there is a great news for you."

Sarah said, "Our wedding dates got confirmed.. And you know what, on 13th October. Rumana & Faizan are getting married, on 14th November me & Shaurya & 15th December, Samarth & Naina.

After hearing this, I asked, "You all planned these dates or it's just a coincidence?"

Shaurya said, "Our parents planned this."

I said, "Oh great Congratulations to all of you. So, next month in going to be very hectic."

Rumana asked, "Are you free today or you have some work?

I said, No, I am free, NO appointments, now a days offseason.

Rumana said, "Then stay here, till evening. We will have fun." I agreed, I again had lunch with them & they arranged a DJ Party at home only. So we danced a lot in celebration till evening the party was on. We enjoyed a lot, drank a lot, danced a lot, ate a lot & then it was time to leave at 7 pm. I departed by saying bye to everyone. I left that place I was on my way to my home I stopped my car at one bear shop & bought 5 cans for myself and again drove towards my house. Parked my car & then opened my flat, entered inside and relaxed myself on my bed. I didn't know why Aaliya is not leaving my mind from past few days. Every minute every second, my mind was thinking about Aaliya only. I opened my laptop. Logged in Gmail I still have that letter which she has sent me on my birthday four years back.

14

Hey Arhaan

Many- many happy returns of the day, God Bless You. Actually I need to talk something with you about both of us. Hope you understand, let me come to the point. In these 2 years of our friendship I never felt such thing for you, as I felt in past 1 month you were not with me in these vacations. Your absence in my daily life disturbed my mind & heart & forced me to think, do I feel the same as you feel for me? But I was getting no answer. As you say there's always a debate between your heart & mind, same happened with me. My heart kept on saying. Its love Aaliya, go ahead & say yes to him. He is the only one for you. Your jallah vallah aashiq is the only perfect life partner for you. But my mind said. No Aaliya you are feeling this because you were not with him for a month. This is just a missing feeling for your best friend. Don't over react on such a silly thing. And you know what; I scolded my mind & told it to keep quiet & supported my heart. My heart happily said, "Arhaan loves you a lot, he will always keep you happy. He will definitely prove himself a good life partner for you. And the best thing is that he is your bestest friend. You both know each other very well, so it's obvious that there will be a good bonding & understanding between you both. He will always respect your feelings & will take care of you with all his efforts. And yes, one more thing, he is the most handsome, charming guy in the college, so you must be proud to accept him as your boyfriend. My heart forced me, "Agree with me Aaliya & one day you will be proud of me."

I thought a lot whatever my heart said to me. These are the exact words what my heart said to me. I couldn't decide anything so now I wanna ask. Whatever my heart said about you is it all correct? Whatever it said, will you follow it? I will wait for your reply, take your own time. You waited a lot for me. Now it's my turn to wait for your decision. You made my birthday a very special one. I made few efforts to make yours too, full of surprises & the busiest day for you. So get prepared.

Once Again, Happy Birthday. ☺

I couldn't believe she wrote this much for me. And if I can understand her heart's words, she is saying a yes to my proposal or she is proposing me on my birthday to make it special 2 years back god gifted me Aaliya as a good friend on my birthday. And today god is gifting me Aaliya as my beloved princes. Her heart is the real hero in our love story & her mind is a miscreant. But finally her heart won & she is listening to it only. She said I am smart, handsome, good looking. I stood up & saw myself in mirror, from top to bottom. I never observed so in myself but for the first time. I was seeing myself from Aaliya's eyes. If she says so I must agree to it. But she didn't clear in last that she also loves me. No, "I Love you" written in the end with birthday wishing. Now what to do? Should I ask? Na, Itna kaha usne, yahi both hai. Mene ese pucha to zyada ho jayega. Let's see her surprises tomorrow. I couldn't wait for the morning to come. The whole night I kept reading that letter with an idiotic smile on my face. This increased my love & respect for her a lot.

My Birthday morning; I never felt as fresh in morning as I felt that day. When Samarth woke up I told him about the letter, he also jumped in joy & congratulated me. Bhaiya & Bhabhi too called to wish me. While talking to Bhabhi, I told her also, what all happened last night. She was happy too.

Now, today I am going to start a new life with Aaliya. If she says I love you too. Then this day will be the most wonderful day of my life I received a message from her, while I was brushing my teeth.

"You fill my life with happiness in many special ways in the quiet warmth & tenderness. You bring to all my days in love you give, in joys you bring in thought fullness in more ways. Then you know I'm so glad you're mine.

Happy Birthday ☺

I re-read the last line. I'm so glad you're mine. Wow But still, I wanna hear it in her voice. I replied with this message.

"Thank you so much. Read your mail last night

I am so happy to read that, very happy to know that you have such feelings for me. ☺

I then sent another message,

"I feel in love with your eyes.

I fell in love with your smile.

I feel in love with your voice.

But most of all

I fell in love with your heart.

Your heart praised me a lot; say a big thanks to it from my side. ☺

She replied, "Yeah, sure, meet you at lunch in mess. After that we will go out. I even arranged out passes for both of us.

I replied with Ok. It was Sunday & usually we don't go for breakfast as we both, woke up late. I then went to the bathroom for shower. I got ready, wore the new shirt, that bhabhi gifted me. It was a purple shirt and blue jeans.

Lunch time was of 1.30 p.m. It was 1 p.m. I locked my room & went down stairs in the central garden. Samarth has already left campus in morning with Naina. I reached the central compound of the hostel. I looked all around, she was not there yet. Then I saw her coming down from the stairs of girls' hostel. She seemed very happy. She was dressed in a complete red Anarkali suit and white stilettos. She was looking awesome. And yes, she was dressed completely in red. I just love the red colour I couldn't elaborate her beauty, I was just staring at her. She was adorable & her smile as always killed me. She said, "**Happy Birthday**," offering her hand for a hand shake. I too moved my hand for a shake, said, Thank you." Hand in hand, we moved out of college, and hired a taxi. She told the driver to take us to Galaxy Restaurant, Naroda. The whole way from hostel to restaurant, her hand was in mine's, fingers locked. Her touch was giving a different kind of spirit to love her.

I wanna go close to her, but it was not a right time & place. I said, "You looking gorgeous today." She smiled & said, "Thank you, by the way you also looking dashing. Nice combination of dress." I smiled & said "Thanks". I held her hand & kissed her on palm. She smiled. We reached the place. I paid the taxi driver & went inside. We entered the lift & she pressed 4 for fourth floor. We were alone in lift. Again, my heart wished to go close to her but I did nothing, just held her close in my arms. We reached the 4th floor. She took me to the restaurant. She was moving & I was following her. We sat on the table the waiter asked for the order & she started ordering. I expected her to ask me as it was my birthday but she herself ordered everything and all my favourites.

I asked her, "How do you know that I wished to eat the same?

She laughed & said "You are my best friend, I know you were well."

I thought she will say you are my boyfriend.

But ....

Waiter came with the tomato soup & served us. And after half & hour we were done with our lunch. After that we had ice-cream, one bowl of ice cream and we two shared that. After that waiter came up with the bill, I saw the bill, it was of 650/- I took out my wallet, but she stopped me & took out money from her purse. How can I let her pay the bill, we argued & finally decided to pay half each.

I paid 350/- & she paid 300/-. Then I asked, "Now what?" She was already having the tickets. I asked "how you arranged it so early?" She smiled & said "With magic".

We then moved out of the restaurant and went to galaxy cinema which was nearby to that restaurant. We entered inside the hall, found our seat & made us comfortable there. The movie was comedy, she was enjoying & I was just watching her expression which were changing with every scene she looks cute when she make faces. I loved each & everything in her. The movie was over at 6 pm. We came out, still hand in hand. I asked her, "Now what, Let's go back hostel" she said, "No, it's too early. We are now going to River Front"

River Front is very far from Naroda. We moved out of the theatre, hired an auto and sat inside. She kept her head on my shoulder and released here breathe as if she was very tired. We reached River Front in 25 minutes. I paid the fare & then we went downstairs to the river front. The benches were at the edge of river. It was 6.30 pm. There was little showering from the clouds up in the sky. That made the evening more romantic Aaliya's hand was still in my hand. Her silky red hair where on her face, I moved them with my fingers at the back of her ear. She raised her head & looked at me. I was not having any word to describe her beauty. The droplets on her hair were looking like diamonds & pearl.

I then moved aside & lay on bench, keeping my head in her lap. She did not offend & started wielding her fingers in my hair. The movement of her soft fingers in my scalp was giving me the feel of heaven. I closed my eyes.

I didn't come to know when I fell asleep, but when I opened my eyes, I was still in her lap. I stood up. It was bit dark all around and there was orange lightening of the solar panels kept there. She smiled at me & said. "You slept for almost 30 minutes."

I checked my watch, it was 7.15 pm, and few men were decorating a table. It was a kind of candle light dinner setup under a lamp. A small area decorated with glittering curtains. As if it was being decorated for a couple. The shade was looking awesome. There were lots of pink roses all around the table; the men were done with their work. A man was approaching us. He said to Aaliya, "Mam, your table is ready. You can proceed towards that." I was not getting anything, Aaliya stood up & offered her hand to me& said, "Come, let's go". I asked, "Where?" She pointed towards that table & said, "There".

I was so astonished to see that the table for two was for both of us. I couldn't believe she did this much for me; she held my hand & took me there. It was truly an awesome surprise for me. I was speechless. There was a bottle of Champagne & chocolate cake on the table. On the cake it was written "HBD to my JWA". She expanded the short form & said, **"Happy Birthday To My Jhallah Wallah Aashiq"** I was really so touched I was getting emotional. Tears were just on the edge of my eye lids, but I controlled myself how could she love me this much? She was lightening the candles around the cake & told me to blow them off. I bent down & did so. She clapped, I took one piece of cake & offered her, she took another & offered me then she handed me the Champagne I never opened the Champagne bottle, but I tried to open its cork in once. I shake it & push the cork with my thumb. Huffff it opened in once. The Champagne flew down. She gave me the glass & poured Champagne in it.

She played a song in her phone. It was a very soft romantic music. It was playing, making evening even more romantic & till then we had our dinner. After our dinner was over, I stood up & then bent on my knees, & asked her to dance with me. She asked for the music.

The same scene from "Kuch Kuch hota hai" I played the same music in my phone & kept my phone on table. She kept her hand in my hand, & then I stood up. A soft dance started in the showering. What a romantic evening it was I pulled her closer. She wound her hands around my neck & my hands were at her back. We were just completely drowned in each other eyes. The fragrance of roses was making the air more & more romantic.

"Nothing could happen much better than this." Suddenly the rain started. The man, who arranged that table, took everything away within the minutes.

Now nothing left there, just us and the rain. She held my hand & said, "Let's go, we are getting wet." I was smiling, said to her "We are already wet now what the sense of going is."

She was trying to move me, but again I pulled her closer. Now there was hardly any gap between our faces. I was lost in her glittering eyes. She closed her eyes then, allowing me to come closer to her. I moved a bit closer & closed my eyes too. My lower lip has touched hers. She moved a bit back & opened her eyes. I too opened my eyes. She again closed her eyes & moved closer to me. I too closed my eyes & held her tightly from back. I felt the touch of her soft lips on mine. We kissed each other for few seconds & she again moved back. After that I hugged her very tightly, moving hands on her back. She held my head. We were completely lost in each other; completely senseless. I left her loose & saw in her eyes, there was deluge of love for me in her eyes. I again moved closer, her lips were beside my ear. She whispered in her sweet voice, "I love you." This echoed in my ears, I looked at her, kissed her cheeks & said, "I love you too" & again I kissed her lips. This kiss continued for almost 5-6 minutes. We broke the kiss after that. The rain has increased. She then requested me to go back hostel. We moved out of River Front & again hired an auto. I checked my watch it was 9 pm we have to reach hostel till 9.30 pm. Aaliya was feeling cold as she was wet, I held her tight in my arms and she too hide herself completely in me I kissed her forehead & said. Thank you". She smile naughtily & bite my ear. I screamed "Oouch."

The taxi driver asked, "What happened sahab?"

I said, "Nothing, you drive fast, we are getting late."

Due to rain, there was a traffic jam on Ambawadi Road. It was 9.20 pm. Our hostel was on walking distance from Ambawadi. Aaliya said, "Let's go by walking. We will reach early". I said, "Ohk". & moved out of the taxi I paid him & held Aaliya's hand. We were walking on the foot path & reached our hostel in 7 minutes. The main gate was about to get close, we entered inside & moved towards the hostel. She was going but I held her hand & asked for a kiss. She smiled & kissed my cheek, "Good night Arhaan. It's too late, let's move". I too kissed her cheek & said "Good night".

I reached to my room; Samarth was eagerly waiting for me only. Samarth asked" Where were you?"

I said "I went on a date with Aaliya".

He asked, "She said yes?"

I replied "No, she proposed & I said "I do"

He jumped in joy & congratulated me then I told him what all, she did for me.

He was happy to know that & said, "I am happy for you dude, finally she is yours now".

I changed my clothes, as I was wet. I was very tired too, so I jumped in my bed. That night was the most beautiful night of my life. I picked my phone & messaged Aaliya "Good night babe. Love you sweetheart. ☺

She replied "Love you too honey. Good Night"

I then closed my eyes with a deep breathe of fragrance & a big smile on my face.

15

The knock on the door interrupted me. It was peon with evening tea. I checked my watch it was 4.30 pm I had my tea & left the office. While I was crossing through Tilak road, I saw a man lying on the road under his bike, his hand & head were bleeding. I stopped my car to help him. I helped him to remove his bike from him & make him stand & helped him to sit in my car. The nearby hospital was Sanjeevani Hospital, I drove towards that. On the way I asked him his name. I told me that his name in Dr. Kshitij Chopra, a Scorpio hit his bike from the back & ran. He was working as plastic surgeon in Delhi & is in Pune for his engagement. I did all the formality in the hospital & admitted him there. He himself informed his family. I said him to take care & left the hospital. I checked my watch, it was 7pm Evening sunset time, and I reached my house. I changed my clothes & prepared a cup of coffee. I sat in the balcony again went in my past. Aaliya was literally not leaving my mind from past few days. What kind of intuitions are these I don't know. But I still love her & I still want her back anyhow.

It was the next day after my birthday.

It was a new morning, a new day & a new life with my angel. A perfect relationship has begun. Our days were going awesome. It was a perfect relationship between us, a perfect understanding; lots of love, care & respect for each other. She used to pamper me a lot and expects the same. After our classes, every hour, she used to send me message "What are you doing honey?" This message always brings smile on my face; make me to feel her love in my heart her presence in my mind, my soul. We use to chat a lot in nights but we talk on phone a few times only. Every night, Aaliya used to talk on phone with her mom. She has a fixed time to talk to her from 9 pm to 10.30 pm I never came to know, what the hell that mom & daughter talks about for one & half hours. I mean on what topic they talk, what they discuss about. Every night I have to wait to talk to her. Sometimes she was tired. Sometimes she has some work to do. One night we were chatting and she was having fever, she hasn't attended college from past 2 days. I haven't seen her from last 2 days. She couldn't come in balcony even, as it was too cold outside. I couldn't go in her room & meet her so were on phone only I was asking her, "You took your medicines? You had your dinner properly?"

She replied, "Ya, I had my dinner, & took the medicines too," I replied, "Hmm, good. How you feeling now?"

She replied". Bit fine. You are there to take care of me. Then I have to get well. Ok now, tell me one thing, why do you care for me a lot?

I replied. "I don't care for you; I am taking care of myself because you are mine only.

She replied with lots of blushes & kisses.

I replied. "Now you sleep, it's too late Ohk".

She texted back, "Ohk, Good Night, Sweet Dreams".

Love you a lot. Missing you I wanna meet you Aaru ☹

I replied Love you too Baby; we will meet soon when you will recover Ohk. Then we will go out for another date ☺ Miss you too Aalu

She didn't like when I call her Aalu, but she has to accept that name because I kept her name "Aalu".

Our 3rd year was towards the end. Month of March is the month of exams. And yes the month of Aaliya's Birthday. Her birthday was on 15 March & our last exam was on 17 March. She already told me not to prepare much; we will celebrate some other day after the exams. But I insisted to meet me on 15th itself. After my lots of request, she agreed somehow between the exams. I managed to buy a gift for her, a black tunic, one piece till knees with a bow on one shoulder & another off shoulder. She was looking so stunning in that. We met near the gate of college she wore that dress for me. After seeing her beauty I was giddy, but controlled myself. We hugged & then moved out of the campus, hired an auto. We were going for just a lunch nothing more than that. On the way, I saw a flower shop & I told the driver in gujarati to stop the auto for 5 minutes.

Aaliya asked me, "What happened?"

I said "just a minute girl. You wait here I just come" & then I moved out of auto towards the flower shop & bought a large bouquet of red roses for her. A tag between the roses, "Happy Birthday Aalu"

"From your love Aaru".

I then told driver to take us to Usmanpura. Aaliya asked me "Why to Usmanpura?"

I replied". We are going for a royal lunch there in Earthen Oven". & then I laughed.

She asked "Earthen Oven??" Before I could say anything the driver interrupted, "Madam It's a very good restaurant famous for its delicious dishes."

The driver said in gujrati & I translated the same to her in hindi.

We reached there in next 20 minutes. I was dressed in blue denim and white shirt with a black blazer that day & she was completely in black and in addition to that a big bouquet of red roses between us. We sat on our reserved table, ordered the cake & then the lunch. She appreciated the lunch & the arrangement I did for her there. Only our table was decorated with red table cloth & balloons. We were done with our lunch. I paid the bill & moved out of the restaurant. When we were moving out, I held her hand & pulled her close.

She said, "Arhaan, what you doing? It's a public place, so many people are here.

I said, "So what, I don't care and by the way, I am not going to kiss you now."

I took her behind a tree, where no one can see us. I make her stand in front of me.

Then I bent on my knees, took out a silver ring from my pocket & said to her.

"Every time I say I love you, I am really trying to say so much more than those three little words.

I'm trying to say, you mean more to me than anyone else in the world

I'm trying to let you know that I adore you & that I cherish the time we spend together.

I'm trying to explain that I want you & that I need you & that I got lost in the wonderful thought every time I think about you.

And each time I whisper, "I love you", I'm trying to remind you that you are the best thing that has ever happened to me.

Aaliya, will you marry me?

She was quiet; tears were rolling down from her eyes in happiness.

I again asked, "Aaliya, will you marry me?

She moved her left hand towards me, allowing me to decorate her ring finger with my ring I held her hand & put the ring in her finger & then I stood up. As I stood up she hugged me very tightly & said "Yes, I will marry you Arhaan. She grabbed me more closely. I wiped her tears & kissed her eyes. Whenever she cries her nose turns red & that looks so cute. I kissed her nose too & then a small kiss on her lips. After sometime, we returned back to hostel. While leaving for our rooms she again hugged me & said "Thanks".

I kissed her hand & said "My pleasure sweetheart". On 17th we gave our exam & on 19th we were leaving our college forever as our graduation was completed. An hour before leaving the college forever we were sitting on a bench in garden. She held my hand & asked very clearly. Arhaan do you really wanna marry me? Will your bhaiya bhabhi accept me?

I too said very clearly" Don't worry about my family, Bhabhi knows everything about us, & I know she will convenience Bhaiya too. Just think about your family, "Will they accept me, your dad, your mom & your sister? She said, "I can convenience my sister & my mom & they only can convenience dad."

I said Ohk. Let's see lets go home & tell our families about our relationship. I really can't live without you, for me it's truly impossible to survive without you Aaliya".

She kept her head on my shoulder & said, "For me too. I love you a lot Aaru," I kissed her forehead & said "Love you too baby".

We then both left for our home. I really don't wanna leave her, but.

A ring on my phone interrupted me. It was 9.30 pm. There was a call from my Boss. He said as I picked up the call, "Arhaan, day after tomorrow, you have to come along with me to Mumbai. There's an important meeting and I really need you there. So be prepared. I will explain you everything tomorrow in office. Is that Ok?"

I said, "Ya, it's absolutely fine Sir,"

I moved out of my room & went to kitchen searched for some food I got nothing more than bread & butter. I had that & went to bed for sleep. But sleep as usual was far away from my eyes.

Our families easily agree with our relationship. We passed out 3rd year too. I got overall percentage 83.4% & Aaliya got 84.4%

Me, Bhaiya & Bhabhi went to Nasik to confront Aaliya's family. We met after such a long time. Our families met. Bhaiya Bhabhi talked to Aaliya, asked her few questions & she perfectly answered everything, Aaliya's mom & dad too talked to me, asked not few but many questions, I too satisfied them with my words.

I spent few time with Aaliya in her room. I bought a gift for her. A silver chain with a pendant of letter 'A' in that. She like that a lot.

I still remember when we were leaving from Aaliya's house, her dad said me very gently.

"Arhaan, you are a nice guy, your family is nice too, but still you have to prove yourself. Get a good post-graduation. You wanna do law then get admission in a good college where you can plant your future, where I can see your secured future. Do something which can assure me that Aaliya will be safe & happy with you.

We will fix your engagement date only after you succeed to get admission in good college. And your wedding will be planned only after you get a job a good job. You can understand why I am saying this".

I said to him. "Yes uncle, I will give my best to prove myself & will rise in your eyes. I will definitely make you assure that Aaliya will be very happy with me.

He kept his hand on my shoulder & said, "All the best". I touched his feet & we returned back to Bangalore.

Now my focus was on to get admission in University of Pune for my LLB course.

It was a very difficult task to get an admission there.

16

It was 3 am. I was still awake my eyes were burning I closed my eyes for a while and made myself comfortable in the bed and fell asleep, I woke up around 8:30 am I knew I was getting late but still I was not doing my work in hurry. I didn't wish to take bath that day so I just brushed and washed my face and changed the clothes reached office at 9:30 AM.

As I entered in the office boss called me and said to meet him in the cabin at 11am. I did the breakfast then checked my mail and it was 11 am by that time I took my laptop and reached to his cabin, he was on phone he told me to sit his face was giving me a weird look as if his wife was scolding him on the other side of phone. He kept the phone saying he is busy.

He then started his discussion with me for almost 4 hrs. He explained me what's going to happen in Mumbai and what all I have to do with respect to that, at 3:30PM I left his cabin and went for lunch while I was having my lunch I again received a call from my boss I picked up and said "hello sir".

He said, "Where are you Arhaan?" I said "In the canteen sir having my lunch" He said, "Sorry to disturb you but meet me again after the lunch, one more thing to discuss don't be in hurry take your time to finish the lunch I am in my cabin only"

I said, "Yes sir sure I'll reach in 15 min" He said "okay" My boss is a humble and amiable personality. He was very impressed with my work and trusts me a lot.

I finished my lunch and reached his cabin again. he was there he said "Actually Arhaan I forget to tell you my son is in pune he came 3 days before from Delhi, yesterday he met with an small accident one gentleman helped him and took him to hospital right now he is in Sanjeevani Hospital I want that you come along with me to discharge him from hospital he is new to this place and needs a company."

As I heard about the accident and the Sanjeevani hospital I recalled about that man whom I helped yesterday I thought to tell my boss about that but then left this thought and went along with him. While we were on our way to hospital he told me that his son is getting engaged after 4 days. Same, that man was also getting engaged soon. The engagement was in Mumbai and after our meeting we got over in Mumbai I have to stay in Mumbai for the engagement party too. So it will be almost 5 days trip to Mumbai.

We reached the hospital and my boss took me to the same man I met yesterday. That man was my boss's son. My boss introduced us with each other Kshitij then told his father that he is the same man who helped him yesterday my boss thanked me for saving his son's life. Kshitij then told me

"Arhaan yesterday I told you about my engagement in Mumbai so now you have to attend my engagement in Mumbai I said "Ya sure I will be in Mumbai only after our meeting.

I took permission from my boss to leave and left the room while I was moving out one girl crashed with me, she was in hurry I fell half down I stood properly and said sorry turning around but till then she entered into Kshitij room may be came to meet him. I too didn't bother, and then I moved to my house from hospital. While I was on my way I called Samarth "Hey Samarth I am going to Mumbai tomorrow" he asked "Mumbai; you going to Mumbai are you sure about this?" I got bit upset and said "Ya there is a meeting and my boss son's engagement so it will take 5 days there."

He said "okay, actually me and Naina are also going to Mumbai after 2 days so you will be there only" I said "that's great "I'll be free at that time" he said "okay done, see you in Mumbai" I said "yeah bye".

Actually there were some memories of Aaliya related to Mumbai. Aaliya used to study in University of Mumbai for her MBA.

I reached my home took out my travel bag packed my luggage for 5 days and kept aside. I turned on the TV, the news channel was showing the revolution of students against reservation few years back I was too part of this revolution I too struggled a lot for my admission in University of Pune for my LLB.

17

After completing my BBA, I applied for my post-graduation in University of Pune. My BBA final percentages were enough to apply online form for admission. I filled the form & was waiting for the reply for admission. Between that time periods, I prepared for its entrance exam. My relationship with Aaliya was also going very smoothly. She applied in university of Mumbai for the MBA through CAT exams. She was preparing for that. We both focussed on our admission & were giving less time to each other.

After a month, I received mail from University of Pune; it was a call letter for admission. I showed it to Bhaiya. He was happy too. I prepared a lot & went Pune along with Bhaiya. When we reached college campus, there was enough crowd, they all were there for their admission only. There was so much of rush, every second person was screaming "that's not fair, the management cannot do like this with us. We want to meet the Director."

I got tensed. I asked one of the boy there he explained that he got a call letter for admission few days back but when he reached there the management said, the seats are full go back to your home, "He asked me for my registration number. I gave him my registration no. written on letter he checked & said "You are also among us ".

I got a shock. How this is possible after waiting there for some time, I came to know that the cut off list was 90% which almost covered 60% of seats & other 25% of seats were reserved of SC/ST/OBC students & remaining 15% was for the girls. That was disgusting. Then why they have sent letters to us, the whole day we all waited there outside the college, but no response from the college management.

Bhaiya said, "Arhaan lets go back, there is no scope, we will find another college."

I said to Bhaiya "No I want this college only. They cannot do like this, we will disrupt all this.

Bhaiya said, "But I cannot stay here for a long time & wait along with you".

I thought for a while & said "No problem Bhaiya, you go back to Bangalore, I will wait here only. I will get admission here only."

Bhaiya knew about my aims, so he allowed me to stay there & said to be in contact & take care of myself. Bhaiya left Pune & I joined the other boys who were doing revolution there. We have told the college system that we will not move from here, till we don't get seats in our applied fields. For 2 days we kept sitting there, we were almost 50 students. For 2 days we discussed about this Reservation Quota in India.

In Indian society because of caste system, Indian has also followed all types of racism & because of this when Indian constitution was drafted the makers of Indian constitution introduced reservation for certain caste & people. Schedule caste & schedule tribes. All political parties know that divide & rule policy based on case & religion will make them rich, will always help them hide their corruption & bad deeds & they are following it religiously.

Today now in India this has become permanent method to give reservation on the basis of caste & religion to get more votes & no-one has authority & power to stop this.

Because of caste systems, millions of families in India got ill treatment & no opportunities to rise in society.

Now we Indians cannot change this without revolt & today revolt is not possible & not good for India. So better is Indians should learn to ask the political parties & as well as tell them we want reservation in everywhere only based on the collective salary of family not caster or religion.

Whatever may be the caste & religion, he is Indian first & poor & weedy he should be given Reservation Benefits.

"Reservation in India" is a hard reality and candidates should understand it, said Supreme Court judge after rejecting the please against reservation. Me & many more like me were expected to understand why a person securing 45.50% was guaranteed seats in Junior college because he/she came from Backward/Schedule class & a distinction student will have to take what available in other fields. With all due respect to Dr. Ambedkar who was after all the architect of the Indian constitution, had aimed to help the oppressed in the society &eradicate castism at that time, years ago. But

I don't think he thought how it would affect students applying to colleges on merit 60-70 years later.

I sincerely hope that there is some kind of relief for the open candidate's students sooner or later because somehow I feel that there is going to be as uprising room.

In the movies 'Arakshan' as the tagline states "Iss Desh me 2 Bharat baste hai". The fight against the quota system & fight for equality will lead to war within the nation, where the situation will be "INDIA v/s INDIA".

They say our friends from backward classes are facing hardship & find it difficult to educate themselves. Well then, why make it difficult for us? Don't we have to give the same challenging exam? Don't we study for twelve hours straight starting at 4in the morning? Don't we deserve a seat that we have worked equally or even harder for?

It was the month of June. The summer was on its heights 3 days have passed. We were still sitting there. Every day Bhaiya used to call me and I give him the report of my surroundings.

One third day of our revolution. One boy stood in centre of our crowd & was very aggressive while saying his words. I could clearly hear him saying.

We should have 10% reservation for Muslims 30% for OBC, SC/ST; like that cricket rules should be modified accordingly. The boundary circle should be reduced for and SC/ST players.

The four hit by an SC/ST/OBC player should be considered as a six & a six hit by a SC/ST/OBC player should be counted as 8 runs. An SC/ST/OBC player scoring 60 run should be declared as a century. We should influence

ICC & make rules so that pace bowlers should not bowl fast balls to our SC/ST/OBC players Bowlers should bowl maximum speed of 80 Km per hour to an SC/ST/OBC player. Any delivery above this speed should be made illegal. Also we should have reservation in Olympics. In the 100 meter race, SC/ST/OBC players should be given a gold metal if he runs 80 meters. There can be reservation in Government jobs also. Let's recruit SC/ST & OBC pilot for air crafts which are carrying the ministers & politicians (that can really help our country). Ensure that only SC/ST & OBC doctors do the operation for the ministers & other politicians (Another way of saving the country)".

That's all what he said. And what I personally thought let's be creative & think of ways & means to guide India forward. Let's shout the world that India is a great country. While sitting idle there, I surfed a lot on Google & came to know that 38% of Doctors in USA are INDIANS. 12% Scientists in USA are INDIANS. 36% of NASA scientists are INDIANS. 34% of Microsoft employees are INDIANS. 17% of INTEL employees are INDIANS. 28% of IBM employees are INDIANS.

Seriously if all those genius IDIOTS had worked for India, we would have raced USA in few years. But I know, this reservation has forced them to serve other counties, their own country don't need such genius champs.

May the good breed of politicians can live long.

I remember, on 4th day, one of the staff of college authority announced that there are 20 seats left. They decreased the cut off percentage to 80%. So the students above 80% can again apply for admission. We all agreed only 10 students went back home. Still 40 were remaining and seats were just 20. Then the college authority decided to conduct an entrance exam. Top 20 students will be selected & remaining 20 have to leave. We agreed to this too. College gave 3 days to us to prepare for exam. I informed Bhaiya about this. He permitted me to give the exam. He told me to go & stay in any hotel & prepare properly. I asked for the examination fees 5000/- He deposited the money in my bank account which I took out from my ATM. I filled the exam form & deposited the fees. In this revolution all around, I couldn't contact Aaliya. Finally when I took the room in hotel, I called her. She hasn't picked. I called thrice; still no response may be she was busy. I was very tired. So I slept I was in a sound sleep. I slept in evening 7 pm & when woke up, I checked my phone; there were 25 missed calls from Aaliya & 5 messages.

Message 1 : Sorry, I was busy with my sister in her wedding's shopping

Message 2 : How are you? Why are you not picking up my call?

Message 3 : Where are you Aaru? Are you alright?

Message 4 : What's wrong? I am calling for 20th time & still no response.

Message 5 : Ohk, Fine, Now I am not going to pick your call ever.

OMG!! Now what to do, she is very angry I called her immediately once, twice, thrice No response. I messaged

"Baby, at least listen to me, let me give the explanation of what all happened."

She called me back. She said "hello." Her hello was having lots of anger, but still she asked, 'How are you? I said "I am fine. Actually I was very tired, so felt asleep in very sound sleep".

She asked where you were from past 5 days." I explained her each &everything which took almost half hour to explain. She heard me very patiently and then apologised for her last message. After talking for some more time, I took bath, ordered some food& started my preparation. I prepared hard for 2 days and on third day morning before leaving for university, I called Bhaiya. He wished me good luck, & I called Aaliya too, she was also my lucky charm. To get admission in University of Pune was very important for me as this will clear my path for mine & Aaliya engagement. This will fulfil one condition of Aaliya's dad "Good post-Graduation."

I gave my exam. The college authority told us to wait for the next day for the results.

Luckily it was my fortune. I was among the top 20 & I got admission there, I called Bhaiya to Pune to do all the formalities for the admission. While we were filling the admission form, they asked for 6 lakhs rupees as donation plus 5 lakhs fees of 2 years.

Bhaiya enquired about the donation fees, 6 lakhs was too much as donation, 5 lakh fees for 2 years was affordable. They said, "Nothing can be done. These 20 students have to pay donation because they are getting admission in extra seats".

Now I under stood their politics, they first rejected those students who were below 80%. Then they conducted exam, now they are demanding for high donation fees, which was affordable for very few & rest will disappointedly go back.

Bhaiya somehow arranged 11 Lakhs rupees for me, I got admission there.

18

My phone was ringing. I woke up from my college past. I saw my phone. My boss was calling. I picked that up, "Hello Arhaan."

I said, "Yes Sir."

He asked, "You are ready to go Mumbai tomorrow?"

I said, "Yes I am ready Sir. At what time should I reach station?"

He said, "Morning 10 is. The train will leave at 10.30 I reserved 2 seats in 1st AC. Reach on time."

I said, "Yes Sir, but why 2 seats, what about Kshitij?"

He said, "Oh Kshitij will come 2 days later.

His fiancée is also here in Pune, so will come along with her later.

I said, "Ohk Sir, I will reach on time."

Conversation ended I saw my watch it was 10 p.m. I felt bit hungry. Again went in kitchen. Just Maggi was there in shelf & a small piece of cheese in freeze. So thought to prepare cheese masala vegetable Maggi for myself. I made that delicious dish with in half & hour, but took just 10 min. to finish that. I was feeling very tired. I have to sleep; otherwise I won't be able to wake up on time in morning. I put earphones in my ears, was listening to soft music & fell asleep. My eyes opened in morning at 7 a.m. The same song was still playing.

I kept my phone on charging & went to washroom for bath. I got completely ready till 9 a.m. I had few fruits & milk as my breakfast. Watched T.V. for a while then locked all the windows & doors inside the house. Unplugged every switch, packed my laptop & locked my house. I gave the keys to my neighbours, came out of apartment & hired a taxi. At 9.55 a.m. I reached the station. Boss met me outside the station as he has also reached there at the same time. We carried our luggage reached to the platform searched out boggy & found our seats. There were 15 min. for train to depart. We were sitting on our seats. My boss said "Well Arhaan I am very tired. I couldn't sleep properly last night due to some work. So I am sleeping now, Ohk."

I smiled & said, "Sure Sir."

I too rested on my seat keeping my bag below my head as a pillow. I have to attend engagement of Kshitij. Every engagement reminds me of my own engagement.

As I got admission in University of Pure for my LL.B degree I mailed my admission letter to Aaliya's dad. He was very happy. He talked to my brother & fixed the date of our engagement. 29th Nov. the same year. 5 months later.

For the 5 months, my mind hasn't set up for studies. I was feeling lonely there as I was surviving without Aaliya & even Samarth too. Aaliya, Samarth & Naina all were in Mumbai. University of Mumbai, Aaliya & Samarth were doing MBA, same class & Naina choose to do fashion designing. Though, I used to chat with Aaliya whole day even during the classes, but still the feeling when she used to sit beside me that cannot be replaced by any other alternatives. Every night, we talk on phone, do video chat. We missed each other a lot. Finally I was about to meet her. I reached Bangalore on 26th of Nov. and she was about reach on 27th Nov. with her family. She came to my home for the first time. We used to live at 29th Lane, BTW in Bangalore. I was so happy, that finally we are getting engaged. Everyone was happy in fact. It was like dream come true. Bhaiya & Aaliya's dad in partnership booked a hotel ITC gardenia. The entire guests were staying there only. We too shifted there for 2 days. I couldn't get a single min. to talk to Aaliya; we both were surrounded with so many people. That was very annoying. I wanted to spent time with her, but nothing can be done at that time.

The engagement was in evening at 7 p.m. I got ready very perfectly. I got dresses in brown bridges, royal blue shirt and white blazer and black shoes, perfectly polished. I reached in the ceremony hall with bhabhi. She was approaching there I could see her from a distance she was looking stunning in saree. Royal blue, silk saree, silver strip blouse & on one shoulder a diamond bow handling her saree. I was just staring her while she was coming toward me. She is truly incredible, her untied hair. So adorable; she came & stood beside me. After a long time her killing smile. Oh god I will faint & fall down.

We were asked to sit on couch kept there. Some ritual activities have to be done. Aaliya's mom did 'Tika' on my forehead and Bhabhi did the same to Aaliya. Then we were given rings, which we have to exchange. Those were platinum diamond rings. So beautiful they were. Bhabhi asked me to put ring in Aaliya's finger. In her ring finger, she was still wearing that silver ring which I gave her on her birthday 9 months ago. I put that engagement ring over that ring only. Everyone clapped & showered flower on us. Then Aaliya held my hand & put the ring in my ring finger. She gave me a naughty smile too. We were happy, very happy. Now no one can separate us. We were engaged now. We had dinner after along photo session. After such a long time, we were having dinner together.

I looked at her, smiled & said. "You looking superb"

She smiled. "You too....."

We laughed but silently. We cannot laugh loudly among so many people

I said, "Listen Meet me after this all get over in the garden."

She asked. "Why?"

I said. "There is a surprise for you. From 3 days we are here, but I couldn't spend much time with you, so will spend some quality time there".

She agreed.

I again said. "Don't change; come in this saree only ok".

She again agreed.

The ceremony was over. Everybody was moving back to their room.

Hiding from everyone letting no one to know, I held Aaliya's hand & moved to the garden. I closed her eyes before we turn towards the garden. We reached there & I opened her eyes. A swing was there decorated with red roses & white orchids. She was so happy to see that & hugged me saying thank you.

We sat on swing I held her hand & kissed that. Again after a long time my lips were touching her. She kept her head on my shoulder. None of us was saying anything. We just wanna feel each other silently. I took a deep breath & then stood up. Bent on my knees & asked her for dance. She gave her hand to me & stood up too.

I said "Aaliya. I wrote a poem for you few days back."

She said "Really. Then say it."

I started my poem.

"Jo dikta hai wo khwab nahi, par khwab sa lagta hai,

Jab khwabo ki pari ho samne, toh dil kaha rukta hai.

Dhunye ki tarah aati hai, jisme na kuch dikhta hai.

Simat jaye ye dhuya mujhme kuch yuhi dil kehta hai.

Yeh bhuri ankhein palko ka parda karti hai

Na khud yeh dekhe mujhko na mujhe dekhne deti hai

Milti hai jab palke ye, naya jahan khulta hai,

Is jahan me hi toh mera jahan basta hai

Kat jaye yahi sari umar, armaan yahi jagta hai.

Jab tum ho bethe pas me kuch yuhi dil kehta hai.

Jab kabhi dekhu tumhe har chiz ye pyari lage

ye gulabi gal aur hotho pe ye lali lage

Bas yahi tamanna jage ek bar chulu inhe

Inhi rango se to meri duniya me rang bharta nahi

Bhar de bas yuh zindagi dil cheekh kar kehta hai

Mita de sari duniya yee faasla kehta hai

Baahon me bhar lu tujhe, kuch yuhi dil kehta hai

Tera noor aankho me liye. Chupaye hai ab tak magar

In aansu ki dhaar par mera na bas chalta hai

Dikh na jaye noor ye, sheesha ke jaise bandho mein

thos kar diya dil yuh, aansu na ab girta nai

Jaane na du tujhko kahi, kuch yuhi dil kehta hai....”

She was in my arms when I finished my poem. After I finished she looked at me kissed my lips& said

"I Love You."

I smiled & kissed her back & said "Love you too."

That whole night we talked a lot. She was very excitingly telling about her college, her new friends. I too told her about my college. I told her that how much I missed her during my classes. I was not habitual to attend any lecture without her. We didn't know when we feel as keep on that swing only in each other arms. It was 5 am in the morning. When I opened my eyes, Aaliya was already awake & was staring at me, with a beautiful smile. I said "The first thing I want to do when I wake up is to see your beautiful face."

She kissed me & said "This all will happen soon"

We then moved to our rooms, that evening she left for Mumbai & the next day I left for Pune.

19

Yes we reached Mumbai. I wake my Boss up. He was in a very sound sleep. I packed my laptop. We come out of station. A cab from the hotel was already waiting for us. We were at Bandra Terminal. And we have to go to Juhu. J.W. Marriot was the hotel. It was exactly in front of Juhu beach. This Mumbai City has separated Aaliya from me. I hate this city. It's truly intolerable to stay here for 5 days but, just for my job, I have to. ☹

We reached the hotel, our room were already booked and I & my boss went to our respective rooms. The next two days, I & boss were very busy with our clients from South Africa. In evening 5 pm our all work was done. Deal was signed & the clients have returned to their place. My boss said "Good Job Arhaan. I am very impressed. Now our official work is done. You are free to enjoy 3 days in Mumbai, go where ever you wanna go, buy all, what you need and just send me the bills." I laughed & said, "Yes Sir, sure".

I left that place & came to my room. Relaxed on bed & turned on the T.V. After a long time, I was watching cartoon Tom & Jerry. I love this cartoon a lot; all others were just sucking creatures. I watched for almost 1 hour. Then tea came within 10 min. I took my cup & sat in balcony. The beach was visible from there the large waves were coming towards the sea shore. Many people were there, enjoying with their family. Some kids were playing, few, not few many couples were there too.

While having my tea & seeing that Juhu Beach, recalled that day when I saw Aaliya for the last time I finished my tea moved out of hotel crossed the road & went towards the beach. I found an isolated place there & sat there on a big rock. That day was 10 Sept. I called her from Pune. I informed her that. I am coming Mumbai tomorrow

Actually she was bit angry on me because we haven't met from such a long time. I was invited in her sister's wedding too, she requested me a lot to come to the Nasik & attend the wedding but I couldn't go due to my hectic schedule in college. But Bhaiya Bhabhi went to attend the wedding. When I said that I am coming, she hasn't believed me. She thought me doing any prank with her. I said "Ok, Don't believe me, when tomorrow you will see me at your own then you will. I will reach till 10am. And the whole day I want you to be with me. Take leave from hostel for 2 days." She said, "Why for 2 days?"

I said angrily, "If I am staying for 2 days, do you have any problem?"

She laughed & said, "No, not at all. I know you won't come. This is just a prank."

I was very happy that I am going to see her after such a long time. After 10 months. I took the train in morning, 6 am, reached Mumbai at 9.30 am. I hired a cab from outside the station for the whole day.

I sat in cab & said driver to take me to the University of Mumbai. I reached there within 30 min. exactly at 10 am from outside the main gate, I called Samarth. He picked up the call. I said "Where are you? I am standing outside the main gate."

He said, "Wait. I am coming there in 5 minutes, within 5 minutes. He reached the main gate, took the permission from guard for my entry. The guard asked for my driving license, after seeing that he permitted me to go in along with Samarth. I was meeting Samarth too, after such a long time. We met like best buddies, hugged each other. He asked me "Where's Aaliya? You informed her or not?"

I said "I told her that I am coming but she hasn't believed me. He laughed & said "No worries. I tell Naina to come here in canteen with Aaliya. The girls will obviously take time to come. Till then me & Samarth smoked & shared many things regarding our college & our future plans of job. He said "I have no other option except to join my dad's business here in Mumbai."

I said "That is not so bad; your dad has great empire."

He said, "Ya, I know". What about you?"

I said, "Job is very important to me. Without job, Aaliya's family will not plan our wedding. I am doing my best, to get a job before finishing my law. I do lots of work, plan so many deals. I stay busy whole day, can't even give time to Aaliya not even to myself. But she understands me so well. She know what I am doing is just for her only.

He asked "And what about Bhaiya Bhabhi?

I said, "Bhaiya got a job offer from Dubai, so he is shifting Dubai for 5 years. And actually I am going Singapore tomorrow for one month. That's why I came here to stay one day with you all."

He said, "Oh, that's great".

At the same time, I saw Aaliya & Naina coming they were at a distance, a bit far. They couldn't see us. Samarth said to me, "Go, & hide somewhere I will also do prank with Aaliya."

I said, "Great idea, I moved & lurked behind a pillar there.

I saw Aaliya coming. I could see the happiness of meeting me on her face. Oh God, her untied silky here, her poised & charismatic face, it kills me every time.

She asked Samarth "Where is Arhaan?"

He laughed very loudly (over acting) & said "Oh Aaliya. You got trolled". I & Arhaan planned to troll you. And now you have been trolled. He laughed more loudly (Oscar winning over acting)" But Aaliya got angry she shouted at Samarth. "What non-sense?" She then took her phone, few seconds later; I saw my phone Aaliya was calling me. I cut the phone. She tried again; again I cut that and typed a message. "Sorry baby, I am little busy now. Will talk to you in evening Love you." She replied "Oh, you are still in Pune & what you have said that you were coming to Mumbai to meet me. Huh"

I then didn't reply. Her face was blend of a pathetic anger. I then moved away from that pillar. Silently came & stood at her back. I then suddenly hugged her from back & kissed her shoulder. She turned around. Her face turned into some nostalgic expressions. Whether to beat me for making prank on her or hug me back for meeting after such a long time. She smiled & embraced me very tightly. She than hit my chest with her fist & said "You are very bad". I said "I am bad?? Ok. I am going back; my cab is waiting outside only." She said "No. I am just kidding baby". We laughed. I asked Samarth about their out passes. Samarth has already arranged those passes and then we all four moved out of the college. We sat in cab. Me, Aaliya &Naina were sitting on the back seat & I requested Samarth to sit in front. The whole day we enjoyed a lot in Mumbai, went to malls did lots of shopping. Ate a lot, drank a lot. Watched movie went to gateway of India. In evening after having our dinner, I then asked Samarth, "Now what, where to go now?" He said "Juhu beach." The girls were shocked & said together "Why Juhu beach at this time, 9 pm?" Samarth said "Don't ask questions, there's a surprise for you all there". We then moved out of restaurant & told the cab driver to drop at Juhu beach. We reached Juhu beach & paid the cab driver for his all day work. As it was late so no-one was there on beach except 2-3 people. Samarth kept his hand on Naina's eyes & told me to do same with Aaliya. I too covered Aaliya's eyes & we moved further.

20

A phone call interrupted me; I came out of that beach night & saw my phone. It was Samarth I picked up the call. I said "Hello" He said, "Hi, your work is done?" I said, "Ya done I am free for the next 3 days. He said "Great me and Naina are reaching Mumbai tonight at 10.30 pm". I checked my watch, it was 8 pm. I asked "You coming by flight?" He said, "Yeah, in which hotel you are staying?" I said, "J.W. Marriot in Juhu." I said "Ok. We will come there; will call you again after reaching to your hotel." I said Ok & disconnected the phone. I order the dinner & again watched the T.V. It came within half an hour. While watching the movie, I had my dinner, after dinner, smoked 2 cigarettes in balcony then moved out of my room. I went out in nearby market to buy few cans of beer; I bought 5 cans & came back to hotel. My boss was busy in the arrangements of engagement. The engagement ceremony was organised in this hotel only. While I was waiting for lift to come Samarth's call came. He had reached the hotel & was standing at reception. I turned around & saw him & Naina. I moved towards them. He was doing the formalities for booking the room. Samarth asked. "Which floor your room is?

I said '4th floor"

He said, "Same our room no. is 407"

I said, "Coincidently mine is 406."

We laughed & then entered in the lift reached the 4th floor. We went to our respective rooms. I was very tired, from last 2 days my boss kept me so hectic, as soon as I fell on bed, I fell asleep. In morning I woke up with the loud knock on my door. Samarth was shouting from outside, "Wakeup, you lazy man, sleeping jerk, Wakeup. I in drowsy state got out of my bed & opened the room door. He shouted, "Its 10 am, you are still sleeping. Don't we have to go for shopping. Get ready fast".

I said "No, I don't wanna go anywhere. I wanna sleep." He shouted. "Stop talking this nonsense & get ready fast, I was not in mood to take bath. I brushed my teeth, washed my face, and combed my hair, changed my clothes, sprayed fogg & then moved out of the room. Samarth & Naina were waiting for me. They were late, just because of me. We were moving out of hotel & they directly took me out of the main gate. We were on road waiting for a taxi; I asked Naina, "What about breakfast?" Samarth turned, gave me very tuff looks & said. "We already did, and you missed that because you woke up late. So now you will directly have lunch at 3 pm, when our half of the shopping will be done. Got it? "I looked at Naina, with starving look at my face she said "Samarth is very hyper right now. Relax, I will do something". Samarth got one taxi & we sat in. They both shopped at lot for their wedding

& we know girls are very choosy for their dresses & especially if it's their own wedding. Naina was very choosing with her every dress. This does not match with your sherwani Samarth. I don't have matching sandals for this, no matching earnings, no nail paint, eye shadow, Oh God. Even Samarth was tired with this matching factor. The whole day I was alive on just chips. Finally in evening we had something in mall & then moved back to the hotel, we reached hotel, with lots of shopping bags. So we kept there in their rooms & then came to the Juhu beach. It was evening; decent amount of crowd was there. Naina said to Samarth "You remember last year, you planned surprise for me here." I looked at Naina, she stopped saying I moved away from them & found a big rock to sit. I took out my cigarette.

21

When we uncovered the eyes of both the girls, they were very astonished to see the surprise, even that was surprise for me too. On the sea shore two tents were fixed & fire was lit in front of them. One tent was for Samarth & Naina and one for me & Aaliya. The whole night we have to stay there in tents. What a wonderful arrangement that was! Aaliya was also very happy to see that. We moved towards our respective tents. One more surprise, there were 2 bottles of red wine, 4 glasses and one guitar too. Samarth hold that guitar & said, "This one I bought for you, gift for you, "I was so happy to see that guitar. My old guitar was too old now to play, I said thanks to him. Naina said, "Not only thanks, have you to sing also while playing this. See what a beautiful night it is."

Aaliya said, "Ya, it's a long time I haven't heard your song."

I gave tuff looks to Aaliya & said, "Every night you sleep after listening to my song only on phone, what it's a long time, 3 days back I sang for you."

She laughed & said, "Ya, 3 days are very long time for me."

We sat there on sand. Samarth made 4 glasses of wine & gave each of us. I vibrated the strings of my guitar & started my song.

"Mere bina me rehna laga hu. Tere hawa me behne laga hu,

Jane me kese, tera hua hu. Mujhe to lagta hai me shayad

Tere dil ki dua hu

Tujhko jo paaya. Toh jeena aaya"

The song was culminated, everybody clapped & Aaliya kissed my cheeks, whispered in my ear, "I love you so much". I said "You always say this only when I sing for you. Now your turn. Say something for me".

She said, "What should I say?"

I said, "Anything, what you feel about me, where I stand in your life something about relationship. Something about our love......." She said "Ok Ok. Give me few minutes to think. I said "Ok I am lighting this cigarette, I will smoke it. The cigarette is over; your time is also over.

She nodded her head in yes.

After 5 minutes the cigarette was exhausted & I said to Aaliya. "Yes, now come on say."

She started her love speech.

"I just can't find the way to express my love for you. You are just amazing in everything. And you always know how to help me in my gloominess. I love you so much. I wanna be in your arms forever, don't wanna leave you ever. Always wanna hug you tight, while I hold you close to me, I totally feel delight. You are the one & always be the one. I will love with all my hearts."

Then she held my hand looking into my eyes & continued, "You entered in my life & made it complete, you held my hand & made me the happiest girl in this world. You stole my heart away with a blink of an eye. Thank you for serving your life with me".

I was so touched with this all she said. I hugged her very tightly. Samarth & Naina started arguing "You never say such good words for me." Samarth said. Naina said. "You never sing songs for me every night." Me & Aaliya laughed, leaving them arguing, we moved inside our tent & closed that. I kept my guitar aside & sat down. She too sat beside me I could read from Aaliya's face, she was feeling bit awkward. I held her hand & said, "Don't worry. I won't force you for anything. My love for you is very pure & I respect your love a lot, so I don't wanna hurt that by demanding any such thing which is not good for both of us."

She smiled & said "Thank you,"

I said, "I also wanna say something to you."

She said "Now what?"

I held her hands, kissed them & said.

"I promise to give you the best of myself. I promise to respect you for what you are, and to realize that your interest, desires & needs are no less important than my own.

I promise that I will honour & protect you as long as I am with you. I promise I will be here with you, like I know you will be there for me."

She was having tears in her eyes, she hugged me very tightly. I fell little back, she said, "You know how much I miss you, every day, every night, every minute, every second, I think about you only. I miss you all the time."

I said, "Actually Aaliya, I haven't told you one thing

She asked "What?

I was very scared to say but I have to say that to her. After gathering lots of guts & I spoke "Aaliya, actually I am going Singapore for one month." She was just seeing me, with blank expressions on her face, not even blinking of eyes; she asked "When you have to go?"

I said, "Tomorrow morning 10.30 am, 11.00am my flight will take off."

She shouted "Tomorrow morning & you are telling it to me now."

Her face was tomato red in anger.

I held her hand & said, "Calm down baby, if I have told you earlier, then you would have got hyper at that time only, & we won't be able to enjoy this much as we did, that's why I haven't told you."

She asked "So for this reason. You came to Mumbai?"

I agreed. She turned around; facing opposite to me, her anger was on its maximum heights.

I hugged her from back, kissed her neck & said, "Baby, I knew you will be angry, but it's important for me to go there. If the team there get impressed by me, then they will give me an appointment letter. My job will get confirmed. That appointment letter will open the door of our wedding. Your dad's second condition will also get fulfilled." She turned around; kept her head on my chest & we both lay down on sand.

She said, "Why you are going so far? I tolerated everything, but going abroad, that too for one month. No, this I can't endure."

I kissed her forehead & said, "I know baby that I don't give much time to you but whatever I am doing, that's all for you only, for our future only. My good job will make my brother feel proud, it will make your dad assured that now you & I will have a secured future. I am doing hard work, not only for myself & you, but for both the families too. My brother & your dad have lots of expectation from me, & that I have to overcome."

She looked at me, kissed my lips & said, "Ya I understand."

I said "Hmm. But you don't worry I will call you. Every day we will do video chat, when I will get free time."

She said "No, no need to call everyday my final exams are approaching next week. So, I have to concentrate there more. One week of preparation & 15 days of exams. Then I will shift permanently to Nasik. So concentrate on your work there & do your best. No need to worry about me, I will manage."

I smiled & said "Aaliya you know you are too good. And I know I will succeed because your love is always with me, which never let me go towards the failure. I love you so much."

She smiled & said "I love you more than anything else in this world."

I pulled her closer, & in that romantic night, we did a very passionate kiss almost for 15 minutes. We were completely lost in each other's arms. That whole night, we were in each other's arms cuddling each other no naughty feeling for each other, just feeling of warmth of love.

In morning when I opened my eyes, Aaliya was already awake. I asked "What's the time?

She said "6 am". There was still little dark. The sun still has much time to rise. She kissed me again & said "Good morning Aaru."

I took a deep breathe; the fragrance of her love was all round.

I said, "I want my every morning like this only."

She said, "It will be, we will get married soon."

We then moved out of the tent. Samarth & Naina were still sleeping. And we couldn't wake them up due to some privacy concern. Me & Aaliya we were walking near the Arabian Sea holding each other's hand. After Samarth & Naina came out of tent, we four moved out from the beach. I have to take bath & get ready to go to airport. So, I & Aaliya went to a small hotel & Samarth & Naina moved back to college. Me and Aaliya event to Santa Cruz & hired a room for 2 hours in the Kohinoor hotel. She was sitting there in room & I went for bath. I came out of bath room, just in towel. She took her eyes away from me. I said to her, "Don't be shy, I am you going to be hubby. This will happen every day after our marriage."

She laughed & gave me my trouser & shirt. I wore that & got ready. She took the comb, held my face in her hand & combed my hair, as if she is combing a small kid. We then checked out from hotel, paid the tariff & moved towards the Chhatrapati Shivaji International Airport. It was 9.30 am. We sat on chair inside the airport.

I said, "Take care of yourself, do your exams well & pray for me that my job get confirmed OK." She kissed my hand & said," Good luck to you too". The announcement was made to go towards the plane. We hugged and small smooch & moved towards the plane. My plane took off.

22

Samarth came and sat beside me. I was still in my thoughts. I said, "Exactly one year, the same day 10th Sept. I have seen her for the last time & till now I am searching for her. I don't know why she left me. For one month when I was in Singapore. I haven't contacted her, for her sake only, but when I returned, everything was lost. I went to Nasik many times; her house was locked every time. Every day I try a phone call on her number, "The number does not exist." Why this all happened to me? Why?? What was lacking in my love? I always showed her the purity of my love. You know Samarth how much I loved her. I cried a lot, my body was senseless, strength less. I fell on Sand. Cried, shouted screamed, louder than the high tides of sea. I just wanted her back anyhow, at any cost, take away everything & just give me back my Aaliya. I will die. I will die.

Samarth held me said "Control Arhaan, control yourself. I know how much you loved Aaliya, but she hasn't loved you. You believe me or not, but she is gone for forever. She is not going to comeback. Forget her & move on in your life."

My pitch was loud, "No, I can't forget her. She was my first love; she was my life, my world."

Samarth made me to stand up. Wiped my tears & took me back to hotel. I came to my room. He gave me some water to drink & then said "Now you sleep peacefully don't think about her much. Ok, Good night."

I said "Ya Good night. See you in morning.

Samarth left my room & closed the door.

I turned on my laptop; I was seeing pictures of Aaliya.

"Looking back on everything, I still remember her smile

I wish things didn't end soon

And tune back time, for while

No matter how much i got hurt

I still love her so much.

A part of me needs her so much

Can't seem to let her go

Knowing I won't be able to see her

Makes my heart cry out in pain.

I can't believe she is not with me anymore

The thought made me wanna go incense.

She was my reason for waking up.

For the smile you see on my face

Going a single day without her,

Makes me feel so out of place."

I was still weeping, lots of tears were rolling down from my eyes and I was unable to stop them. But then I thought.

"Over thinking ruins you. Ruin the situation twists things around, makes you worry & just makes everything much worse than it actually is."

Those silly conversations we had, those nights where we stayed up late talking to each other. I miss them all, every one of them. I still remember our one conversation.

Aaliya "You know what kind of wedding I want?

Me: "No, what kind of?"

Aaliya: "I've dreamt of a big wedding, in a place filled with flowers & friends

Me: That's nice

Aaliya: "Hmm, so what kind of wedding do you want?

Me: One that would make you my wife

I closed my eyes; few more tears rolled down from my eyes & then fell asleep. In morning I woke up with call. Call from my boss. I attended the call. "Good morning Sir" My boss said, "You still sleeping Arhaan, it's not morning, its afternoon, see the watch."

I saw my watch, it was 12.30 pm afternoon. I said "Oh I am sorry sir." My boss laughed & said. "It's alright. I just called you to remind that tonight there is the engagement ceremony in the party hall. The party hall is on 7th floor. So, reach there by 8 pm ok.

I said "yes sir, I will reach there.

My boss said. "By the way, Kshitij wanna meet you so he is coming to your room within half an hour.

I again said "Ohk sir, no problem.

He then kept the phone I moved out of my bed & then called Samarth. He said he was in market with Naina.

I got fresh, took bath, got ready. My laptop was lying open on my bed. I packed that, & then I heard a knock on my door. I opened & yes it was Kshitij. He said "Hi, how are you?" I said "I am fine, what about your injuries?" He said "I am also fine, & my injuries are well now."

I asked him "Sir said you have some work with me, what was that?"

He said, "Oh yeah, actually I wanna buy a gift for my fiancée, so I need your help can you come with me to a nice gift shop lets buy good present for her"

I thought for a while & then said "Ok fine, let's go. I have no work to do whole day my friends also went market."

He asked "Your friends?"

I said "Ya my friends, they came Mumbai, 2 days back for their wedding shopping He said, "Ok let's go"

We went to market, around the Juhu & Boriveli all malls we roamed, but he was so choosy, he even didn't know his fiancée's likes & dislikes. Finally he bought a silver necklace. Coincidently Samarth & Naina were in same mall & they found me. They came to me & I introduced them to Kshitij. Kshitij said, "Nice to meet you. Today's is my engagement so you two also join the party along with Arhaan Ok."

He continued "Ok Arhaan thank you so much for help. You enjoy with your friends, I am leaving, and you all reach on time. Ok Bye."

23

In evening three of us reached the party at around 8.30 pm so many guests were there. The decoration & arrangements were too good. We three found a table and sat there. I heard a voice calling me from back. "Arhaan" I stood up & turned around, it was Kshitij beside me. Kshitij said "Meet my fiancée, Aaliya my Aaliya, I clearly heard Kshitij saying, my fiancée Aaliya, How could she be his fiancée, she was mine. I looked towards Aaliya. She was too stunned, shocked, senseless and expressionless seeing me. Kshitij said." Aaliya, this is Arhaan, the man who saved me in Pune. He works in dad's company as a Legal Advisor." Aaliya haven't responded to him. We both were just staring each other. So many questions were rising in my mind. How to ask? Why she was getting engaged to Kshitij?" I was seeing her after such a long time, exactly after a year.

Kshitij said, "Ok guys, you enjoy the party. He then turned to Aaliya & said," Let's go honey."

My ass burnt, how he can say honey to Aaliya, my mind was saying "Go Arhaan, hit him hard, he touched your Aaliya." But then I stopped, because

Aaliya too turned & went along with him. Samarth said. "Arhaan, that was Aaliya she is getting engaged to your boss's son, I couldn't believe" I looked towards Naina. Naina ran behind Aaliya but she was lost in crowd, & after that she got busy in the ceremony I saw her putting ring in Kshitij finger & Kshitij too put ring in her finger. That was the third ring which was going in her ring finger.

I couldn't tolerate all this happening in front of me. I just needed the answers of my questions, which only Aaliya can answer & she is getting engaged to someone else, in front of my eyes. I drank a lot & then moved out of that party hall. I was completely senseless in sub-conscious state; Samarth held me & took to me to my room. I was in giddy state. In morning when I woke up, I saw Samarth & Naina, sleeping on the couch in my room. As I woke up they woke up too. I was feeling so restless that I was unable to stand up even. Samarth asked me. "How are you feeling now?"

I asked in shock "What has happened to me?"

He said, "last night, you drank a lot. Then you fainted. Your blood pressure was very high & you have fever too. Doctor came for your check-up & gave you 2 injections, so that's why you are up now. Otherwise you would have slept forever."

I asked, "What's the time?"

Naina said, "Its 2 pm. Let me order the lunch. You have to take medicine after that." I said "No, I don't wanna have anything. Where is Aaliya? I wanna meet her."

I tried to stand up, but I fell on bed as my legs were having no strength.

Samarth shouted at me, "Just sit her quietly. There's no need to go anywhere. Have your lunch and take your medicine."

I said, "No, I wanna go, I again tried to stand up but Samarth pushed me back on bed & I lay down on bed. My head was bursting in pain. Naina gave me a glass of water, I drank that. After that lunch came, I was not willing to have anything I just wanna go to Aaliya. I just needed the answers of my questions. But Samarth coerced me to have lunch. I had little & then took the medicine. Samarth pointed her index finger towards me & said in anger "Don't move from here we are coming back. The whole night I was lying on this couch. I need to get fresh."

I nodded my head & he moved out of my room. As he left my room, I tried to stand up again. I couldn't but still I tried. I moved out of my room. Silently, went to reception & asked the receptionist. "Can you please tell me the room number of Ms Aaliya Juneja?" She said, "Sorry Sir, she is not in hotel right now. She will return in evening." I hit the desk very hard. The receptionist got scared. I said sorry to her & moved out of hotel. I went towards the beach. There was no sun visible in the sky. The clouds have trapped it. The weather was stormy. It was about to rain. Wind was blowing heftily. I sat near the water on sand. All those questions were hitting my mind badly, punching my soul from very inside. I was lost in infinity. I heard an amicable voice, "Arhaan" I looked right, and she was standing beside me. I raised my head to see her. I then turned my face away from her. She sat beside me. For next 10 minutes, none of us said anything. Then she spoke, "You should not have done this to me. Why you cheated me Arhaan? Why you left me? What was my mistake? You haven't tried to contact me even for once.

I was shocked to hear all this. This was what, that I was about to say. How can she ask me like this?

I said, "Excuse me. I haven't cheated you. You cheated me. You left me; you haven't tried to contact me in past one year. I searched for you everywhere all over the Mumbai & Nasik. In past one year, I became an insane, dying in your memories. I returned from Singapore with my job appointment letter, but when I reached your home nobody was there. I asked your neighbours. They didn't know anything I enquired in your college, useless. I asked Samarth & Naina they also didn't know anything. While I was in Singapore, where you got lost after your exams were over. Where were you?" I shouted in very loud pitch.

She was crying after a while. She wiped her tears & said 2 days after my exams were over, I went out for shopping before coming to Nasik. I bought lots of gifts for everyone, for you also. I was having lots of bags in my hands. While I was coming to the main road to catch a taxi from other side of road, a truck hit me very badly. After that when I came in conscious state, 7 months have passed to my accident and I was in Delhi AIIMS hospital. The first name came out of my mouth was yours, my dad told me, that he tried to contact you, but couldn't. He went Pune in your search he couldn't find you there even, not even in Bangalore. He couldn't contact any of my friends because my phone got lost in accident & all contacts were in it. Your bhaiya bhabhi were also not there in Bangalore.

They shifted to Dubai. No source to contact them also. And you say I cheated you."

I was very much shocked to hear all this. She continued saying. "My head got hurt very badly, it got operated for 4 times and due to which I was in coma for 7 months. It took 2 months to me to get normal. Last month we turned to Nasik and now I am able to live a normal life. Still many complications are there in my body."

I was weeping, hearing all this from her. Now she shouted, "Now you tell me where you were from past one year?"

I wiped my tears & said, "When I was in Singapore, 2 days before leaving to India my phone got stolen. I lost my phone in Singapore and I couldn't stay there in search of that. So I returned back to Mumbai. I bought new phone & a new SIM, the first call I dialled was yours, but I didn't succeed. Whenever I try it always says, "The number is currently switch off. Please try after some time." I then I came Nasik directly from Mumbai. Went to your home, the house was locked. I asked neighbours, they didn't know anything. I again came to Mumbai, went to your college, no information about you I got from there. Now you tell. What could I do in that case?"

We both were silent, after 5 minutes. She spoke, "Your phone was stolen. That's why dad couldn't contact you & my phone got lost during the accident, that's why you couldn't contact me. This was reason; we couldn't reach each other & just suffering from one year.

I said, "I am still waiting for you, and you got engaged to someone else, I trusted my fortune & you couldn't wait for me, you lost trust on my love.

I have never expected that I will see you in your own engagement that too with a third person, why are you getting engaged to Kshitij?"

She hasn't replied to me. I again asked." Tell me why you decided to marry that guy. Say something. This engagement ring of Kshitij, has replaced my two rings that I gave to you."

She was still quiet, and then she stood up & went away. I too stood up, "Aaliya, Aaliya wait. Where are you going? Answer me; you cannot go like this, leaving me in this trap of questions. You have to answer me. "She hasn't listened to me she moved out of the beach. I followed her. She entered the hotel & caught the lift. I tried to reach her, but failed I came back to my room. Samarth was standing there. I looked at him & went inside my room. He asked me, "Where were you? I told you not to move from your bed.

I said, "Aaliya came to meet me when I was at beach." He got shocked & asked. "You talked to her? What she said?"

I narrated each & every sentence of mine & Aaliya. The same question he asked, "But why she is getting married to that Kshitij? Now you are back then what the reason that she didn't answer & left that place.

I said, "I don't know. My head is bursting." Samarth gave me a tablet & then I slept. The next morning we all checked out from hotel. I saw Aaliya's parents there standing in lawn. I approached them, but then I saw, Aaliya, my boss, my boss's wife & Kshitij were too standing there. So I stopped myself & moved out of hotel. I left the company ticket & went along with Samarth & Naina. I reached back to Pune, to my house. I was very tired, so I slept, setting the morning alarm of 7 a.m.

24

The next morning I woke up on time & got ready to go to office. The whole way while I was driving to office just one question was in my mind which was left unanswered, was still hitting my head, my heart, and my inner soul. What could be the reason behind it? I know her love was not a fake, I know Kshitij could not love her more than me in just 3 months. My 4 years of love was much more powerful than any other bond. Then why she broke that. Huh"

I reached office parked my car & went in. I reached my cabin; few files were already there for my work to do on them. My room phone rang I picked up, it was from my boss. He asked "Hello Arhaan. Are you there in office?" I said, "Yes Sir, I reached half an hour ago." He said, Ok, I am coming to your cabin & kept the phone down.

After 10 minutes, he came to my cabin. I stood up. I was shocked to see Aaliya along with my boss. I wished him, "Good morning Sir."

He said, "Good morning, Arhaan, meet my going to be daughter-in-law, Aaliya. She is an MBA from University of Mumbai. She will work with us for the next 2 months, till she gets married to Kshitij." She is new here for everything. So, it's your responsibility to teach her & make familiar with everything. It's your duty now. I am handing her to you. Ok."

I said, "Ok Sir, No problem."

He said to Aaliya, "I hope you will enjoy Arhaan's company. He is a nice guy. So you stay here with him & I am going back to my work. My boss then left my room. Now only I & Aaliya were there in my room.

That question I tried to ask her but my phone rang, one of my clients, I moved out of the room to talk due to some network problem. When I was over with the call & returned back to my room. She was holding the photo frame which was kept on my table. There was our engagement pic in that. She sensed when I came in, kept the photo frame back on the desk & moved out of the room. We were working together, every deal. She used to discuss with me. I tried a lot to get the answer of my question, but every time, she avoided me & moved away. Samarth & Naina too tried to talk her about this, but she hasn't said anything to them, also. I don't know why she was quiet on this. Each & every passing day was killing me. My tolerance power got over. Finally I wrote a note for her.

"I don't hate you because you left me,

I hate you because you said you would never leave,

I don't hate you because you made me feel this way.

I hate you because I never wanted to feel like this again in end.

I hate loving you. Dam, I loved you </3."

I kept that note on her table & left the office. Came to my house, I lightened my cigarette & sat in balcony. Now I was regretting on my words that I wrote for her. She will get hurt after reading that.

Doorbell rang. I went to open the door. It was Aaliya there. With that note in her had. I got scared. What she was about to say.

I told her to come in & she came in & after that I closed the door. She was in very much anger; I still can read her face. She said, "You wanna know why I am getting married to Kshitij, even if you have returned to my life?

I said, "Yes I want answer to this."

She said, "Because my parents want so, Kshitij is treating me from past 1 year. He loved me, he saved my life. He gave me a new birth. He did lots of hard work on my treatment. I don't know when he started liking me. He talked to my parents that he wanna marry me, because only he can understand my physical condition & only he can make me overcome with my injuries.

My parents told me all this. I refused without thinking for once. I just loved you, only you. I could let myself go, in somebody else's life that was truly impossible to me. My dad tried to convince me a lot. He said, "Come on Aaliya, Kshitij is a nice guy, he likes you. He loves you a lot. He is well settled good family background. I am sure he will keep you happy & will definitely make you overcome from every bad thing.

Kshitij was so nice to me & my family. For the 10 months he treated me so well & hasn't asked for a single penny for the bills of hospital. Not even my dad was capable to pay such a huge amount of bill of hospital. My parents begged me to say yes to Kshitij. They even said, "Arhaan will never return, mark our words. He left you, he cheated you. He went Singapore & got settled there only. His family too left this country. He was fraud, forget him & start a new life with Kshitij."

I was left with no option. I have to marry Kshitij for my parents' sake."

I fell on couch restlessly. I sat beside her, held her hand & said, "I will pay for everything don't worry about that I will talk to your parents, I will show that I am not fraud. I will explain them that what all happened to me in Singapore. Please, leave Kshitij. Marry me Aaliya, I will die without you. I love you......

She was crying & then said, "I love you too, but now I couldn't leave Kshitij. First I got engaged with you, and then we got separated. Now I got engaged to Kshitij. Now you are saying that I should leave him & marry you. No Arhaan. I couldn't do this. This will raise a big question mark on my character. Sorry I couldn't marry you Arhaan. She stood up & moved out of my house. I tried to stop her, but she sat in her car. I reached to the window of the car & said "Listen to me Aaliya, nothing will happen."

She said, "I don't wanna listen anything tomorrow I am leaving Pune forever & going Mumbai in a wedding, Kshitij cousin is getting married & after that I will go to Nasik. From now we are strangers, forget me Arhaan. Good Bye. Take care of yourself. Then she left.

I got filled in anger. No sense of requesting her this much. Fine I also don't need her. I can survive without her. I don't love her any more.

25

For the next 10 days. I tried hard to move her out of mind. But that was truly impossible. How can I let her go like this? But my all trials were waste. She will not convince at any cost. She doesn't want me, back in her life. Now what I was supposed to do??

There's one thing I've learned in life is to fight, fight for what is right. Fight for what you believe in, what's important to you. But most importantly, fight for the ones you love & never forget to tell anyone how much they mean to you, while they're still alive.

I will fight for my love. I will go Mumbai. I will try for one more time. My love cannot culminate like this so easily. I called Samarth, Naina, Faizan & Shaurya to come to my house immediately. They all reached within half an hour. Faizan asked, "What happened, why you called us in so urgency?"

Shaurya said, "You seem to be tensed. Say what the matter is?"

I said, "I want Aaliya back. She is getting married to Kshitij & I can't let this happen. After 5 days she will get married.

Naina said, "She is not getting married after 5 days, she is getting married tonight. She re scheduled her wedding day.

I was shocked, "How can she do this? I wanna go Mumbai right now?"

Shaurya said, "How can you go Mumbai right now?"

I said, "I don't know anything, I can't let her marry someone else, I am going.

I left my house, sat in my car & drove very fast toward the airport. I checked the time in my watch. It was 5 pm. I reached airport. All others were following me in another car. I parked the car ran inside the airport. I went to the enquiry counter.

I asked, "Can I get a flight of Mumbai right now?"

The lady sitting on counter, I am sorry Sir; you can't get a ticket of Mumbai right now. The flight took off just 5 minutes ago. The next light is a 7 p.m. You have to wait till then.

Damn, I missed that. No other option except to wait here till 7 p.m. Samarth said to me, "Don't get mad. Where will you find her in Mumbai, how can you convince her now, just few hours of her wedding?"

Naina said, "She is in the same hotel. I am trying to call her, but she is not picking up the call."

I checked my watch, it was 6 p.m. I went to ticked counter & bought ticked for myself. Naina said, "I will also come with you to Mumbai. It will be easy for you to convince. I agreed. Samarth too permitted her to go along with me.

I got the tickets. We sat in flight & it was about to take off. In those 20 minutes, when we were in flight, all the memories flashed back in my mind, which encouraged me more to stop her. We reached Mumbai. We came out of airport. It was raining too much in Mumbai, it was the month of November, and still it was raining heavily. We were in Santa Cruz & we have to go to Juhu. We asked so many autos & taxis, but they all refused to go, due to heavy rain. We roamed all around the airport for almost an hour, but didn't get anything. Finally we got a taxi & requested him to take us to Juhu, he agreed. We sat in. Due to rain there was a huge traffic jam on Milan Subway. The distance from Santa Cruz to Juhu was about 5 kms, and we got stuck in traffic jam. There was lots of water on roads. I checked my watch it was 8.30 p.m. Naina was still trying to contact Aaliya, but no response from her side. We spent almost half hour in that traffic. I asked the driver, "How much long in this traffic jam?"

He said, "Sir it's very giant, don't know when it will move, Juhu is 2.5 km away from here. If you can, then please go by walking. I also wanna go back to my house. It's very late Sir."

I paid him & we moved out the taxi. We were finding the way to move out of those vehicles. Horns, horns & horns, there was lots of water. I & Naina were running on roads. The wedding time was of 9.30 p.m. and in watch it was 8.45 p.m. I was running like hell, Naina was too following me. I was so lost in running. That a bike hit me suddenly I fell on road, & that biker said me blind & moved away. Naina helped in getting me up. My hand was bleeding. Naina took out my handkerchief from my pocket & tied it round my palm. We again ran & finally reached the hotel. J.W. Marriot. The hall was decorated. I was in very bad condition. Just in a trouser & a shirt. Wet in rain & wound on hand. I then asked the location of Aaliya's wedding.

The location was on 5th floor, mid-lawn. We ran towards the lift. The lift was busy. I checked my watch it was 9.15 p.m. I said Naina, "Leave this lift, we will go by stairs, come."

We ran towards the stairs, we were climbing in a very hard condition. Naina was tired. She couldn't climb now. I held her hand & reached the 5th floor. Even I couldn't breathe properly, as if my lungs & nose got chocked. I told Naina to ask someone, when we could find Aaliya. I saw Aaliya's sister there. I ran towards her & she was shocked to see me in such a bad condition. She asked, "Arhaan you here?"

I said, "Didi, please tell me, where is Aaliya, I wanna meet her. I wanna stop this wedding, she can't do like this to me."

She said, "You can't do like this to her. You can't stop her wedding."

I said, "Why not? I know she won't be happy in her life. She is doing just a compromise by getting married to Kshitij. She is destroying her own life, Kshitij life, my life. You know very well how much she loves me & how much I love her. Then how can you let her marry someone else, whom she does not love.

I didn't notice but Aaliya's parents were standing just behind her sister. I moved towards her dad & said, "Why you did this uncle? Why couldn't you wait for me? You said, get a good graduation, and get a good job to prove yourself. I did everything. But you are you giving Aaliya's hand to someone else. Pune is not a big city. You could have easily found me there, but you didn't trust me. You were not having belief that I can achieve something, that's why you forced her to marry someone else, who was already settled."

Her parents were quiet, their eyes were down. I said again, I won't let her marry someone else except me. I will stop this wedding, tell me where is she? Her sister said, "Come with me, I will take you to Aaliya". I went along with her & she stopped in front of Aaliya's room & allowed me to go inside. I went inside. Aaliya was sitting there, alone. She was facing a mirror & saw me standing back through that mirror. She turned shocked to see me. She ran towards me & said, "Arhaan why you came here, just go please somebody will see us. Please go."

I held her hand & said, "I will go, but I will take you also along with me. I won't let you marry Kshitij.

I wanna marry you. I know you still love me. I know you are not at all happy with this wedding. Then why are you destroying yours, mine & Kshitij life. No one will say anything. I talked to your parents too. Come let's go."

She was quiet, she was weeping. I asked, "What happened? Let's go." She moved her hand back. She moved few steps back & said, "No, I can't."

After saying this much to her, she is still saying no. I got hyper. I said, Ok Fine Destroy your life, destroy my life & destroy Kshitij life too."

She said, "Listen Arhaan, I can't go with you. What I will answer him. He will get hurt."

I said, "Oh so you care about him more than me. What about me. I am getting hurt from last 1 year. Don't worry about Kshitij. I will talk to him and I am sure he will understand.

She said, "He saved my life, when I was about to die, he cared for me for 7 months. I was unable to walk; he held my hand & made me stand on my feet again. He was always there with me when I needed him. I can't cheat him like this at this critical time."

I got more hyper & said. "So, you wanna say that my love, my care was a fake. I was never with you when you needed me. If I knew about your accident & if I could reach you at that time, I would have done much more than this."

She was about to say but I stopped her & continued, "Now I will not come, stay here, get married. I am going, sorry that I loved you so much & waited for you." I then left that room & moved out of the hotel.

26

The last chapter is narrated by Aaliya.

I did not know that Kshitij was outside the room and heard our conversation. As Arhaan left the room, Kshitij entered in. I was shocked to see him. He came towards me and said, "All that I did was just my job. I am a doctor & to take care of my patient is my duty. Your parents offered me the marriage proposal that's why I agreed, thinking that you are a nice girl."

I was shocked & asked him," What? My parents came to you?"

Kshitij, "Yes"

Me, "But they said you like me and you wanna marry me."

Kshitij: "What? I never said like this to your dad. He himself approached me for the marriage.

I was not getting anything why dad played this game with me. I called my dad and asked him to come in my room.

He came. Mom & my sister were also there.

I asked my dad, "Why you did this dad? Why you lied to me? Why you played with my life?"

He said, "Beta. I thought of your welfare only. I thought Arhaan cheated you he will never come back. I knew you won't think about any other guy except Arhaan, that's why. I knew he is in Pune, but I haven't told you. My eyes were stuck on Kshitij only. I saw him taking care of you, he is well settled. That's why.....

I was speechless. What to say him.

Kshitij said to my dad, "Uncle, you were about to destroy three lives. That man is not a fraud; he is still waiting for Aaliya, searching for her from past 1 year. He truly loves Aaliya."

Then Kshitij said to me "Go Aaliya, go & get him back otherwise he will go very far and then you won't be able to get him back go Aaliya, don't waste time.

I ran out of the room. I was still wearing that bridal dress. I ran out of the hotel. I saw Naina there. Naina came towards me & asked "Aaliya you here? What happened?"

"Naina, where's Arhaan?" I asked

She said, "Don't know, he just left without saying anything & told me to reach airport after 2 hours."

Oh God! Where to search him now?

I said Naina to go airport. It was 11.30 pm. It was raining; no vehicle was there at that time. I was in dilemma, from which direction should I start searching for him. I was thinking where he might go at this time.

Suddenly my mind clicked, I ran towards the beach. I searched everywhere but I could not see him. I moved around half kms. It was dark all around &

raining too. I was searching for him all around. He was not there I lost hope. I turned, and as I turned. I saw him sitting at the sea shore, crying loudly I ran towards Arhaan & stood beside me. Seeing me there, he stopped crying & stood up.

Getting out of control in love is not bad always. Sometimes it is needed to show your love. A gesture to show your love that how much that person mean to you. A sudden kiss is a best example.

I held him tight & kissed him for few seconds. I wiped his tears & kissed his eyes then, as he used to kiss my eyes, whenever I cried. He smiled & hugged me very tightly. Again, after a long time, I whispered in his ear. "I love you."

He looked at me & said, "I love you too."

And then we kissed, Oh God! What an awesome zest it was.

Happy End